D1317473

TREASURES OF THE WORLD

COLLECTION PLANNED AND DIRECTED BY

ALBERT SKIRA

TREASURES OF SPAIN

FROM ALTAMIRA
TO THE CATHOLIC KINGS

INTRODUCTION BY
F. J. SÁNCHEZ CANTÓN
Director of the Prado, Madrid

TEXT BY
J. M. PITA ANDRADE
Professor at the University of Granada

SKIRA

Translated from the Spanish by Isabel Quigly

★

© 1967 by Editions d'Art Albert Skira, Geneva
Library of Congress Catalog Card Number: 67-25118

★

Distributed in the United States by
THE WORLD PUBLISHING COMPANY
2231 West 110th Street, Cleveland 2, Ohio

★

PRINTED IN SWITZERLAND

CONTENTS

FRANCE

San Salvador de Valdediós
Santillana del Mar
Santander
Oviedo
Pindal
Bilbao
Santa María de Naranco
Altamira
Puente Viesgo
ASTURIAS
Santa Cristina de Lena
Pamplona
Pilgrimage Road to Santiago de Compostela

Santiago de Compostela
GALICIA
Perpignan
NAVARRE
Talull
San Pedro de Roda
Pontevedra
León
San Miguel de Escalada
Erill-la-Vall
CATALONIA
Miño
Astorga
Sahagún
Burgos
ARAGON
Cardona
Vich
Gerona
Paredes de Nava
Quintanilla de las Viñas
Manresa
Tarrasa
Pisuerga
Palencia
Santo Domingo de Silos
Lérida
Cogull
San Pedro de la Nave
Valladolid
Duero
Soria
Saragossa
Barcelona
Sabor
Zamora
San Juan de Duero
Ebro
Douro
El Burgo de Osma
Tarragona
LEÓN AND CASTILE
Tortosa
Salamanca
Coca
Sigüenza
Limit of Moslem territories at the end of the 11th century
Avila
Segovia
El Paular
Valltorta
BALEARIC ISLANDS
MINORCA
El Escorial
Guadalajara
MADRID
Teruel
Palma
Tagus
Toledo
Valencia
MAJORCA
Alcántara
Bicorp
IBIZA
LISBON
Guadiana
Játiva
FORMENTERA
PORTUGAL
Villena
Elche
Alicante
Cordova
Murcia
ATLANTIC OCEAN
Guadalquivir
Los Letreros
Cartagena
Huelva
Seville
Granada
Kingdom of Granada at the end of the 13th century
Lebrija
Almería
Málaga
MEDITERRANEAN SEA
Cadiz

INTRODUCTION

Instinct may lead certain animals to work, to build, to organize themselves, but man alone has the faculty of sustained initiative, of improving and perfecting his works. This means that he has been able to satisfy his needs and tastes, and has made contact with forces greater than himself, whose power he recognizes and even to some extent controls.

In this all-important fact lies the seed of all the arts, and it must be ascribed to man's ability to think, which, together with the power of speech, is his most distinctive quality in the natural scale. Man's development was very slow, of course, and today we know that his time must be measured in millions of years. We have come a very long way from the time when the Irish bishop Usher calculated that 4004 years elapsed between the creation of the world and the birth of Christ.

The reader who admires the figures of animals painted with such mastery in the cave of Altamira will note that, as the text rightly says, they are "without known antecedents." The accent must be placed on the word "known," because quite certainly works as fine and as complex as these were preceded by drawings, paintings and reliefs on perishable materials that time has destroyed.

Among the very large number of prehistoric cave paintings that have been preserved in Spain there are some that are astonishingly good, with a wonderful range of decorative motifs and methods. No archaeological explanation is needed for them; they exist in their own right as works of art. How numerous and how varied are the artistic means employed in them is clear from the book's first pages, and this "multiformity" is something constant in the development of Spanish art. Paradoxically, it leads one to consider the "inconstant" elements in Spanish art as well.

"Simultaneous variety" and "frequent change" are phrases that might well be applied to the situation, for Spain, as the link between western Europe and Africa, shutting in the Mediterranean and facing the islands of the Atlantic and the lands beyond it, was open to every influence from outside. And, since geography conditions history, the Iberian peninsula was a meeting place, a land of clash and interchange and transition.

It is hardly surprising that soil so thoroughly tilled should bear fruit of the most varied kind. Sometimes the ordinary cycle of artistic development came first, but failed to achieve much; a particular style would be hinted at, would fail to take hold and only later would come to fruition, as if it had been brought in from outside. This happened, for instance, in the case of Romanesque architecture.

Professor Pita Andrade's essay makes these general ideas quite clear; but, as both author and publisher have done me the honor of asking for them, I shall add some remarks of my own to the most interesting of his.

Prehistoric Spain expressed itself artistically in three ways: in painting, in dolmen architecture, and in gold and silver work (leaving aside ceramics). The first two of these developed in particular areas, at least so far as we can judge today, but the third extended over almost the whole of the Peninsula—a fact that is easily explained by the facility with which objects made of rich materials can travel.

The realistic paintings of animals in the caves along the northern coast, and found to some extent in central Spain and even, very occasionally, in the south, are quite unlike those of eastern Spain, where scenes of everyday life are depicted in caves and shelters. The bison, horse and wild boar of Altamira foreshadow the vivid naturalistic feeling of the great Spanish painters from the Renaissance onwards, but the "phallic dance" of Cogull (Lérida), and the picture of the man taking honey from the bees in the Araña cave (Valencia) show the taste for minute, everyday observation later to appear in medieval altarpieces, wall paintings and illuminated manuscripts. Without pressing the point too hard, there are similarities to be found in the twelfth-century artist who, on the tympanum in the vault of the Royal Pantheon in San Isidoro in León, shows two goats munching buds off a branch; or, to mention only one example out of hundreds, in the son of Master Rodrigo de Osona, who early in the sixteenth century shows a bullfighting lance in the background of one of the paintings of the altarpiece of San Dionisio in Valencia cathedral. In the Renaissance, too, an artist who knew Italy, Pedro Machuca, shows a boy with his head bandaged in his *Descent from the Cross*, in the Prado. This liking for everyday aspects of life may explain why Flemish painting was welcomed in fifteenth-century Spain, and it must also explain the vulgarity of certain characters and scenes in the Spanish classical theater, even at its highest level.

Of prehistoric architecture, only funerary monuments appear in the present selection. The rest scarcely counts, from the artistic point of view: a few menhirs, such as the one at Gargantans (Pontevedra), which was certainly also funerary; a few rows of standing stones, a few cromlechs, a great many fortifications, and the mole at Vares (Corunna). Spain has megalithic monuments of impressive size, such as the so-called Cueva de Menga at Antequera (Málaga), which is 80 feet long with a span of 20 feet at its widest point; it is in the same district as the Cueva de Viera, which is also megalithic, and the Cueva del Romeral, which has walls of rough masonry but is roofed with large stones, both in the passage and in the tomb chamber itself, the roof of the latter consisting of a single enormous stone. Beside the tomb chamber is a smaller room—an arrangement also found in the much finer tomb at Mycenae known as the Treasury of Atreus. These monumental constructions are entirely undecorated, except for the dolmen of Soto (Huelva), which has repetitive line reliefs carved on stones so large that in times to come men wondered how they could have been moved into position. It need hardly be said that there is no similarity or connection whatever between this unadorned architecture and later developments in Spanish art.

Gold and silver work, unlike painting and buildings, could be brought into Spain quite easily from countries in the Near East and in the North, both in prehistoric and, above all, in early historical times. In studying this work, the art historian is always faced with the problem of determining, in the case of any particular piece, whether it was imported or made in Spain, where there were large gold and silver mines. The considerable number of treasures found, most of them in what seem to have been hiding places, gave rise to legal prohibitions against treasure hunting, and royal decrees were issued to this effect in the seventeenth and eighteenth centuries. In modern times fewer treasures have come to light, but important finds have been made at Caldas de Reyes (Pontevedra), El Carambolo (Seville), and Villena (Alicante).

From the end of the second millennium B.C. the Peninsula, with its wealth of metals and crops, became increasingly attractive to the peoples living around the shores of the Mediterranean. Repeated expeditions were made to Spain. At least it is from this time that they are authentically mentioned, although the ancient texts that refer to the riches and advanced culture of Tartessos still present many problems; in particular, its exact position has never been determined. Artists working in metal, and particularly in gold, achieved an astonishing degree of skill. Gold was mined in abundance in places like Galicia and Asturias, where the oldest ornaments have been found; they are extremely heavy, but jewellers soon began to make the most of the metal itself, both there and in the south and east of Spain, by doing embossed work, filigree work, and granulated work. Extensive research needs to be done before a comparative study of all this jewelry can be made, and before the many elements found contemporaneously in it can be seen for what they are, and their respective dates established. The forms which immigrant peoples brought with them were not always substantially different from those they found in Spain, since before they arrived there, from the Near East or from the North, they may have been in contact with others who had been to the

Peninsula, or whose products had reached there. The Celts are often considered at the same time as the Phoenicians or the Greeks, but this may often be misleading, for a number of currents are often mingled in Spain.

A study of the many statuettes of women discovered in eastern Spain and the Balearic Islands helps in considering the gold and silver work of the first millennium B.C. The reader should examine the illustrations carefully, and in particular the most beautiful example of Spanish art of the time, the Lady of Elche, although this is far from being the unique example that many people consider it. In these sculptures the eastern influences plainly seen in many Spanish works of art down the centuries are evident, together with obvious Hellenic influences.

The settlers in the Peninsula were so varied that there was little solidarity among them until the Roman conquest, which was not easily achieved. North Africans were probably the oldest immigrants, followed by waves, large or small, of Iberians, Celts, Phoenicians, and, in smaller numbers, Cretans and Greeks. The Peninsula's incorporation into the Roman Empire had great and even glorious results in the political and above all in the literary field: Spain produced emperors, and some very fine writers, the greatest in what is called the Silver Age of Latin literature—Seneca, Lucan, Martial. But the development of its visual arts was not comparably splendid.

Admittedly, within the farflung Roman Empire no aqueduct compared with that of Segovia, no bridge excelled those of Alcántara and Mérida, and no lighthouse that of the Tower of Hercules at Corunna. But these are engineering works, stamped with the practical Roman character, not works of art. The many buildings dedicated to the gods, the commemorative buildings and those used for games and spectacles, have no local character of their own, and Spanish architects were clearly not seeking to give their work a particular aspect within the general framework of Rome.

This is also true of Roman sculpture in Spain. There is plenty of it, and of high quality. Much of it, including large sarcophagi, was no doubt brought from Italy and other provinces of the Roman Empire. I am not convinced by the arguments put forward to suggest that it was made in Spain, although there are exceptions, such as the sarcophagi found in the Alcazar of Cordova and in Tarragona, whose reliefs have a dramatic force that seems peculiarly Spanish. The Sarcophagus of Hippolytus at Tarragona was found underwater, near the shore, but as we do not know whether the ship carrying it was sunk when it was landing or setting sail, we cannot be sure whether or not it was made in Spain.

There was no unity in the Peninsula, then, until the Roman conquest; and there was no independent life, with its own government and laws, until the rule of the Visigoths. In his recent book *L'Espagne du Moyen Age*, the distinguished student of Spanish and

Arabic history, M. Henri Terrasse, describes the situation very clearly: "Medieval Spain's destiny was quite unlike that of its neighbors in western Europe. After the upheaval of the Germanic invasions it had a long period of stability: the Visigothic monarchs, having soon lost their hold on Aquitaine, extended their authority over the whole Peninsula. Under their authority, Spain had the advantage of political unity for 293 years. Religious unity was established under the Catholic Visigoths, and a unified system of laws was gradually achieved. Earlier than Gaul, Britain or the Germanic countries, Spain enjoyed a civilization that for its time was brilliant and in many ways original, and, in the twofold feeling of its own unity and its own personality, found the beginnings of true Spanish patriotism." The Visigothic contribution in Spain, thus authoritatively stressed by this learned French historian, has not always been recognized.

The vigor of the new Spanish nation meant that artists tended to hark back to forms that had been cultivated in Spain before the coming of the Romans, and still persisting: the horseshoe arches found on tombstones in León, for instance. Visigothic art was formed from these elements and others that came into Spain with the gold and silver work from the North, based on the Roman tradition that immediately preceded them, and combined with others from the strong Byzantine empire, brought in by settlers in the East and South.

Thus, as always, Spain attracted art forms from outside and ended by fusing them with its own. The question of which came first often arises, as, for instance, in the case of the horseshoe arch found in many Hispano-Roman tomb reliefs. When seeking to establish its origins Professor Pita Andrade hesitates to attribute them definitely to the horseshoe arches of Visigothic architecture, or to those used in Syrian churches: but the proximity of the former would seem to weigh in their favor.

It is perfectly clear, and the evidence cannot be disputed, that in the early Middle Ages Spain again became a field of artistic interchange between the East and the lands of Western Europe; and this was so both before and after the important period that opens in 711, with the coming of the Moslems.

Recent studies, which give the exact numbers of the early Moslem expeditionary forces, arouse astonishment and incredulity. Manuel Gómez-Moreno, the leading scholar of this period, gives us the facts: "Twelve thousand Berbers under Tariq," he writes, "ten or eighteen thousand Arabs under Muza, and seven thousand Syrians who came later, in 741. Altogether, thirty-seven thousand men at the most." The political and military structure of the Visigothic kingdom had been weakened by internal dissensions and was easily swept away, but at the beginning of their occupation of Spain the Moslems respected the social structure and even the religion of the Visigoths.

Only thus can the most important meeting of East and West in the Iberian peninsula be explained. The way in which such unexpected factors came together to form Spanish medieval art is explained in the text and made clear through the illustrations. The variety and novelty of the means used to bring such widely separated elements together is quite clear; and so—to take only the main examples—is the way in which Moorish and Mozarabic architecture developed. In the nineteenth century, writers like Juan Valera were already emphasizing how much the Moorish civilization of Spain owed to the physical features and peoples of the Peninsula. But today, with our much fuller knowledge, we can evaluate the collaboration of East and West more precisely.

Yet the idea of collaboration cannot be used without reservations: often it was a case of taking over buildings or parts of buildings, as with the original mosque of Cordova, which is thought to have owed something to the Visigothic church of San Vicente; and, of course, complete elements, such as Roman columns in Moorish buildings, were taken over too. Another historical factor that must not be forgotten is the presence in Spain of a great many Jews, who no doubt helped the Moslems to arrive and to settle, in those early medieval centuries. The concourse of so many peoples, all so varied, produced a wonderful, multiple, untidy vitality that is reflected in the arts of building and decoration, as in no other western country.

These and other historical comments go beyond the scope of this book, but they may serve to stimulate the reader, and even provoke objections and arguments—which are all to the good, since reading that leaves the reader quite passive is generally valueless. Professor Pita Andrade, who knows medieval architecture so well and is so restrained in all he says, does not hesitate to suggest the likely origins of Spanish art, although he knows perfectly well that what matters is the work of art itself, however significant scholarly inquiry may be.

The buildings that seem to anticipate the full Romanesque style, and suggest there were earlier Spanish buildings that did so, and the way in which the initiators of Gothic architecture used Moorish intersecting arches and rib-vaults, needed to be pointed out and evaluated, as well as explained.

Although it has been said very often already, Spain in the Middle Ages had two groups of visitors, each very different from the other and coming from very disparate places, yet both bringing in very much that was new and spreading abroad much that had been born and bred in Spain. These were the pilgrims to Santiago de Compostela, who began arriving in the ninth century, and travellers drawn to Moorish Cordova by its fame and splendor in the tenth century. Much has been said about what was brought into Spain along the Road to Santiago, but little about what Spain sent out that way to the rest of Europe. The influence of the Crusades on the development of architecture has probably been exaggerated in the past. Rough warriors were not necessarily better educated than the pilgrims who followed powerful lords, many of them men of culture and even patrons of the arts, to the shrine of St James. When they passed along the roads of Spain, when they visited churches and monasteries, they must have been astonished to find artistic forms they had never seen before; many visited the Cámara Santa of Oviedo on their way to Compostela, and the pre-Romanesque buildings in Asturias, León and Galicia must have made a deep impression upon them.

The development of the great Moorish, Romanesque and Gothic styles of architecture is shown in the admirable illustrations with commentaries, which make further explanation pointless. A few passages from M. Henri Terrasse's book, already quoted, showing aspects of the Spanish Middle Ages that generally pass unnoticed, may be useful, however. The ideas put forward by this French historian, which stick closer to documented facts than many of ours in Spain do, may help to modify Spanish views on the War of the Reconquest, which lasted 781 years.

"Until the eleventh century Spanish Islam, with its advanced, many-sided civilization, ought to have made the full weight of its influence felt in Christian Spain, which was small and poor. And yet Christian Spain was influenced by only a few forms taken from its art and spread by the Mozarabs. Spanish Islam never deliberately sought to spread Islamic institutions and artistic forms created in the emirate and caliphate of Cordova." "Islam could not conceive of these peaceful conquests: to Islam, the world was divided into the *dar al-islam*, the kingdom of Islam, the kindred country where all changes were possible, and the *dar al-harb*, the rule of war, where the faith of the Prophet must be spread with fire and sword." "It was Christian Spain that, through the Reconquest, learned to love the civilization of the conquered Moslems, to adopt what its own faith allowed it to take, and, sometimes, to pass on to other countries, near or far, these involuntary links with Islam."

M. Terrasse's clearsighted remarks are deepened by further observations of his: "It was the Reconquest that allowed a fertile symbiosis," he says, but adds: "These fusions were as much the result of military advances as of deliberate policy." "Spain used a rare tolerance towards its Moslem vassals, respected their faith, their law and their customs and took over some forms of life and art from its conquered brothers, in a friendly way." "The policy of the Christian kings was basically inspired by the sense of a Hispanic unity that Islam had not been able to abolish, and by the wish to find this unity again, beyond the difference of faith." "To the wish to reconquer... must be added the spirit of Spanishness, a certainty that Spain was not merely a geographical and ethnical unity, but a collective awareness as well..." "This lucid and brotherly tolerance meant that Spanish art kept a destiny and an aspect all its own until the end of the Middle Ages." These wise remarks should be widely considered, and deserve our gratitude.

My comments, though not systematic, may do something to give the reader an idea of the characteristics of Spanish art in the many centuries before it became fully incorporated into western art. This happened first of all when the fully formed Romanesque style penetrated Spain through the Cluniac foundations, and then when Gothic building began, with the Cistercians. It would seem that, in the field of Spanish art, Christians and Moslems clashed harshly but fruitfully, for, as García Gómez wrote, Islam both stimulated Spain, and acted as a counter-irritant.

Professor Pita Andrade's specialist knowledge appears in the chapters on Romanesque sculpture and architecture, and it would be pointless to try to add anything to them. What he says about wall painting and illuminated manuscripts and, later, about panel painting might need detailed consideration, but an introduction is, I feel, hardly the place for this.

F. J. SÁNCHEZ CANTÓN
Madrid, March 1967

ON THE THRESHOLD
OF ART

THE LADY OF ELCHE. WHITE LIMESTONE. ABOUT 4TH CENTURY B.C. PRADO, MADRID.

How many thousands of years must we go back before we find Spain's first treasures? When can the works of the earliest inhabitants of the Iberian peninsula be called artistic creations? These two questions are very hard to answer. Standards established by man lose all meaning when applied to those early days. Errors of judgment may add up to centuries, one way or another. We shall never know when or where the first work of art was produced. But we can say that the creative activity of human beings that led to the first cultural advances we know of took place in southwestern Europe a very long time ago.

Spain is one of the few countries privileged to show evidence of these decisive activities. Man was, through art, moving away from the other animals, and crossed the boundary beyond which things have a meaning greater than their own mere usefulness. Thus a process began that has continued into our own time, and was owed to exceptional individuals. Genius is apparent in the oldest works of art, though it may be found in a group, incorporated in some collective effort.

Looking at Spain's early art, and choosing representative works from among its treasures, one is struck at once by the remarkable historical role of this country, situated as it is between two seas and two continents. For several thousand years Spanish art was constantly changing, though time must be measured very differently in the Stone Age and the Ancient World. It was not like Egypt, for example, where forms appear to have been static. The Iberian peninsula gives abundant proof that it was in contact with other civilizations in ancient times, and perhaps this is why its artistic heritage seems so remarkably varied. The works accumulated from the Palaeolithic to the Middle Ages show highly interesting links with those of other countries.

When most of Europe was covered with a huge ice sheet, Stone Age man was found in Spain because of its milder climate. Near Madrid, in the valley of the Manzanares, remains survive from the Lower Palaeolithic Age, with flint axes that are, in fact, pre-artistic treasures. We must come much nearer our own age, though still twenty thousand years away, to see the birth of art in the Upper Palaeolithic Age. It is in this period that the development of cave painting began, progressing through a series of stages that take us across the Neolithic and actually bring us to what is called the Bronze Age, within the second millennium B.C.

No country shows so complete a panorama as Spain in the field of cave painting. For this reason highly representative examples can be chosen to identify the phases of an artistic evolution that leads from realism to abstraction. In this way we can, across nearly twenty thousand years, link up works made when man lived in the most rudimentary way, as a hunter, with others made at the same time as those of the Middle East, when the Mesopotamian and Egyptian cultures were at their height.

In order to complete the picture of primitive man's activities, creations of other kinds would have to be collected. For instance, in the wide field of the household arts, one would pass from the Palaeolithic bone tools to ceramic work of the Neolithic Age, which shows much more highly developed social structures. The birth of architecture, too, could be seen in megalithic monuments. But the way in which Spain's relations with the large centers of the Mediterranean area influenced Spanish art is much more important, for these connections explain the profound changes that altered its whole way of life.

Contact with the great Middle Eastern cultures gave a character to many works that contrasted with others in which Nordic elements appeared. The conflict between disparate influences was to reappear again and again throughout Spanish history; and even in the Ancient World, Spain symbolized, through its art, the eternal struggle between East and West.

When the Greeks came as colonizers and the Romans as conquerors, the Iberian peninsula finally became a part of the classical world. Paradoxically, it was through its eastern shores that it became linked with western civilization. And it was as part of this civilization that Spain was to enter the Middle Ages fully formed. Many thousands of years were to pass before the country acquired its character, many centuries reflected in rich, varied works of art. The paintings that appear without known antecedents in prehistoric caves, the pure elements crossed with other, outside elements, the final acceptance of classical forms, suggest that the broad, early stages of Spanish art were a basis for what was to follow: developing always on the threshold of art.

THE CAVE PAINTINGS

In 1879 Don Marcelino Sautuola, an eminent scholar from Santander, made a spectacular discovery near Santillana del Mar, on the northern coast of Spain. As he was searching for prehistoric objects in the cave of Altamira, discovered eleven years earlier, he was astonished to find paintings on the ceiling of a wide low room, a side cavern to the left of the entrance. They were first noticed by his little daughter, who was with him. In a pamphlet published the following year he wrote that he considered these works to be primitive. But, as nothing similar was known in Europe, scholars at the time almost without exception poured scorn on Sautuola's idea; and he was even thought a fraud. Years later, after his death, new discoveries confirmed the importance of Altamira, which the French scholar Salomon Reinach felicitously called "the Sistine Chapel of prehistoric art."

Even when compared with many important later discoveries, Altamira still remains the first great treasure of Spanish art. On the ceilings of the cave we see Palaeolithic painting in its most complete and characteristic form. According to present-day estimates, the earliest paintings are reckoned to be about twenty thousand years old, corresponding to the Aurignacian period, and the most recent about eight thousand years old, within the Magdalenian period. The most primitive drawings show the development of a few primary forms, though they seek to be realistic; human figures, on the other hand, are only sketchily suggested, by anthropomorphic outlines. These hesitant forms give way to others, in the Magdalenian period, that are full of plastic vigor. These show such realism, such sureness of line, such effects of chiaroscuro conveyed through colors, that it is hardly surprising that Altamira finally became an early symbol of what was destined to happen in Spanish painting thousands of years later. On the other hand, the art of this cave may be not so much the oldest example of a national style as the first glimpse contemporary man had of his distant ancestors' capacity for artistic creation.

Nearly all the Altamira paintings are concentrated in a very small space. The cavern is about sixty feet long and less than half as wide. The roof slopes towards the far end and from a height of six feet to slightly over three. To allow visitors in, the floor has had to be cut out. In one very narrow corner, the artists cleverly took advantage of the irregularities in the rock and, in the course of many generations, drew animals there with no sort of order, sometimes superimposing them on others, and sometimes leaving them unfinished. It would appear, from the densely packed figures, and the character of the paintings themselves, that this picture gallery was a kind of sanctuary; the whole cave is several hundred yards long and much wider in parts. In painting these animal pictures, primitive man may have been trying to make his hunting successful. This

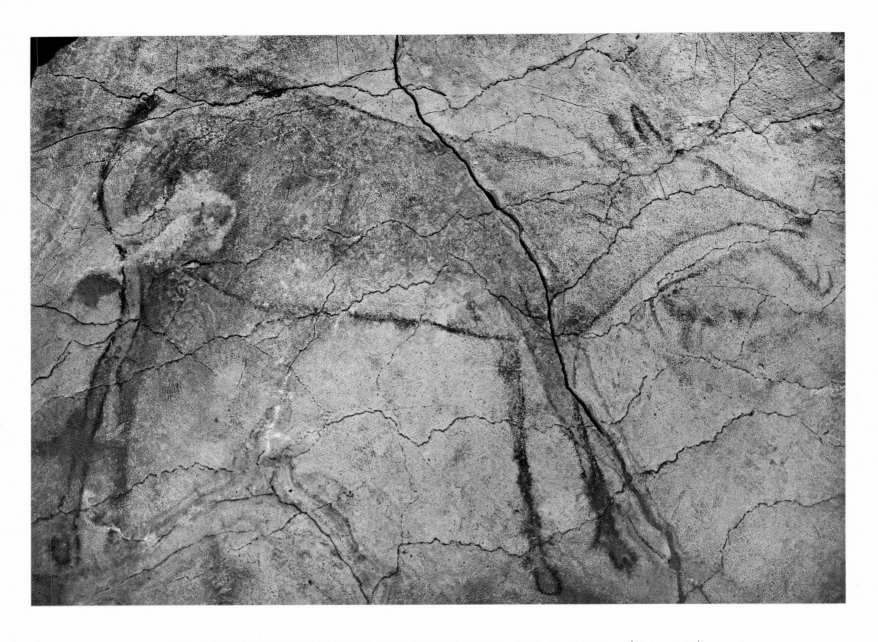

DOE. PALAEOLITHIC CAVE PAINTING. MAGDALENIAN PERIOD. CAVE OF ALTAMIRA (SANTANDER).

magical character stimulated the painters, who showed remarkable powers of observation and skill in the use of the most varied techniques. Most of the effects at Altamira are produced by the drawing and the colors, but there is engraving as well (figures scratched in outline on the rock) and the artists took advantage of the uneven surface of the ceiling to get effects of relief. It is surprising, too, to see the painters expressing themselves in a far more bold and radical way than later painters were to do. The bison, wild boar, horse, and deer are not only shown with profoundly naturalistic features, but caught at a particular moment, and with astonishing expressiveness. It is in this that the special quality of these paintings lies, in their unprecedented ability to translate the artist's creative urge.

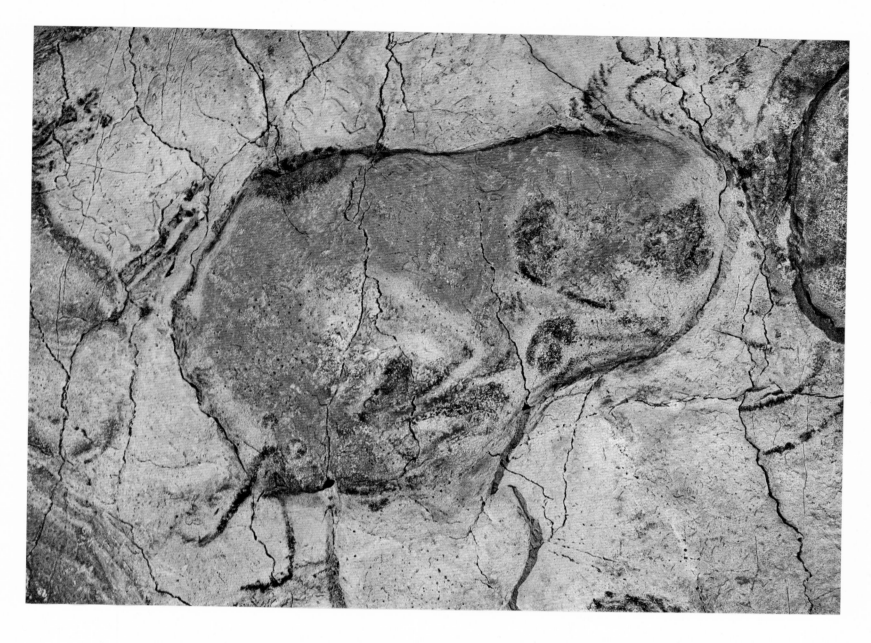

BISON. PALAEOLITHIC CAVE PAINTING. MAGDALENIAN PERIOD. CAVE OF ALTAMIRA (SANTANDER).

From the animals of Altamira we can imagine the conditions of life of Stone Age man in the south of France and the north of Spain. The cold, which was still intense, forced these men to shelter in the caves for most of the year. During the long winters they fed on what they hunted in summer or on short excursions outside; and spent the rest of their time fashioning tools of stone, bone, ivory or reindeer horn, and drawing and painting these magically-intentioned animals.

The animal most often painted is the bison, a worthy ancestor of the Iberian bull. There are nineteen fair-sized bison at Altamira, represented in the most varied forms and attitudes; resting or moving, in outline or with the head turned sideways, showing four well-differentiated legs or with a fifth leg included to give a better sense of movement. The effects achieved with color are remarkable; red and black predominate. It is in the pictures of bison that the irregularities of the rock are most cleverly used to achieve a feeling of relief. The finest example of powerful movement is the bison that appears timid, with its head turned away, yet ready to charge, and admirably revealing its controlled energy. But there is none more realistic than the female in heat, lowing anxiously, with her neck stretched out.

The vital energy of some of the other animals at Altamira is equally striking: a pregnant deer, for instance, resting; or the wild boars, one of them walking, with eight legs drawn in to give a sense of movement, and another, drawn in black strokes and with heightened effects of chiaroscuro, running with its legs very wide apart; or with a speckled technique that shows up the outline. In every case it is clear that these wonderful artists had outstanding gifts of observation.

No Palaeolithic cave paintings surpass those of Altamira in quality. And in spite of many later discoveries, the greatest example of Magdalenian art is found there, just as the greatest example of Aurignacian art is found at Lascaux. But this must not blind us to other important discoveries in northern Spain. Their abundance, and their connections with those in France, led the Abbé Breuil and other prehistorians to include them in a large artistic zone they called Franco-Cantabrian. The term is not exact, however, because Palaeolithic paintings have been found in the south of the Iberian peninsula: for instance, in the cave of La Pileta, in the province of Málaga. For this reason it would be better to designate this art as Franco-Spanish or Hispano-French.

Among the caves in the Cantabrian district it is worth noting those at Puente Viesgo, a few miles from Altamira. Their special value is that they show a very large number of forms and styles, covering long periods, in paintings scattered about the caves some distance apart from one another. Some of the animals there, such as the elephant, are not found at Altamira. But what is newest and most radical in the paintings is the human element. In the cave of Castillo were found the outlines of hands, in reddish and black tones, that belong to the Aurignacian period, and on top of them there are sometimes representations of animals that belong to later periods. These drawings are not so important artistically, but anthropologically they are extremely valuable. In some cases the fingers have been mutilated.

Outside the province of Santander, in Asturias, there is something worth noting in the cave of Pindal. Here the outline of an elephant is drawn, with a mark at the height of the thorax. Was the artist trying to show the heart, through a transparent exterior? If so, this would be the first known representation of it; and if the interpretation is correct it has the added interest of appearing in a datable work of the early Aurignacian period, involving an animal that was very soon to disappear from Spain.

IMPRINT OF A HAND. PALAEOLITHIC CAVE PAINTING. AURIGNACIAN PERIOD. CAVE OF CASTILLO, PUENTE VIESGO (SANTANDER).

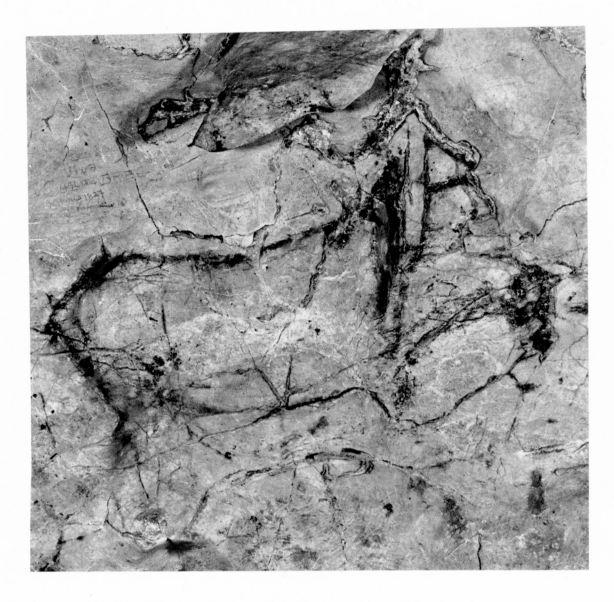

SHE-GOAT. PALAEOLITHIC CAVE PAINTING. CAVE OF PINDAL (ASTURIAS).

The art of other caves amplifies the whole panorama of cave painting. For instance, an analysis of the engravings found at El Parpalló (Valencia) or at San Román de Candamo (Asturias), of the Solutrean period, and the highly interesting ones at Los Casares (Guadalajara) show the expansion of Upper Palaeolithic art into the center of Spain. Indeed, the whole of the Iberian peninsula gives examples of the first great chapter of cave art, which was also so highly developed in France.

Palaeolithic painting in Spain is followed by a series of remains found in a wide area extending from Catalonia to Andalusia, which give its peculiar character to the prehistoric art of eastern Spain. Today nearly all the experts agree that this came after the Magdalenian period. The findings are very important. The paintings are not located in deep caves but in "shelters," hollow rocks that can be seen in the open air. These works are very poorly preserved and many have survived only because of the dry climate. They are in strong contrast with Palaeolithic art. They show small figures, which very often form scenes. As a rule they are monochrome, red predominating in various tones, and to a lesser degree black and other colors. The urge towards realism, which we admired so much in the earlier paintings, is no longer found in them. What counts is the outline, which is full of movement. But what is most important and new is the appearance of the human figure, which means a great step forward in the history of art. No longer do we find anthropomorphic signs or traces of hands. Man is shown in the shelters of eastern Spain in the most varied forms and attitudes: in most cases, hunting with spears and arrows; in others, which seems seriously symptomatic, fighting against other men. This means we have reached a cultural state developed enough to make war a subject for iconography. Finally, the human figure is represented in scenes of erotic content that suggest the rite of procreation.

There is no doubt that the world in this eastern part of Spain was very different from that of the Palaeolithic caves, and much nearer our own. But it is impossible to connect this painting at all clearly with what has been found in North Africa. Perhaps future discoveries will allow us to see the art of eastern Spain in the context of the early cultures of the Mediterranean. Today we can merely assign it to a period of transition, called the Epipalaeolithic, with a date somewhere between 6000 and 4000 B.C. Nevertheless, new discoveries continue to be made further inland and further south. Can these be the first artistic signs of the first socially organized peoples in the Iberian peninsula? Were these the people who ceased to be hunters in order to develop the much more complex forms of life found in the Neolithic Age?

The techniques, styles and ideas found in the painting of eastern Spain all forcefully suggest a period of transition. Thus they link two worlds as distinct as those that conditioned life in the age of chipped stone (Palaeolithic) and in the age of polished stone (Neolithic); and, in addition, they are links in a chain that brings us almost into historical times. The important discoveries are found mainly in five provinces of Spain: Lérida, Castellón de la Plana, Valencia, Teruel and Albacete. In Cogull (Lérida) is one of the most interesting from the thematic and artistic point of view, although it is in a very poor state of preservation. Near some animal figures is a group of women, who have very drooping breasts and skirts to their knees; they are dancing round a completely naked man. The scene's erotic character is obvious. The human figures are represented in the form of stylized silhouettes, and their outline is what mainly counts. These paintings were initially red, and later touched up with more vigorous strokes of black lines.

In the cave of the Caballos de la Valltorta (Castellón) the hunters facing the deer show the fine sense of movement that is characteristic of the artists of eastern Spain. There is great variety in the attitudes, besides, and even the effort the archers are making in shooting off their arrows is apparent. The outlines of the animals are drawn with great delicacy. In the cave of Araña, near Bicorp (Valencia), there is a picture which, if it has been correctly interpreted, may be unique of its kind: a man, climbing up ropes, has reached a hive and is collecting honey in a pot while bees are buzzing around him. Lower down, and also tied with ropes, is a highly stylized human figure. The pot and at the same time the activity of these men bring us to a more advanced cultural stage than that of the hunting peoples of the Palaeolithic Age. This is yet another sign of the transitional character of the art of eastern Spain.

Further into the Sierra de Albarracín (Teruel) new aspects of eastern Spanish art appear in works where the figures are more stylized, with extremely simplified animals and archers. Martín Almagro has observed how in the shelter of Doña Clotilde the idea of landscape is suggested by a tree, represented with roots, leaves and fruit.

Finally, in the province of Albacete, many aspects of the prehistoric painting of eastern Spain are reflected in the discoveries at Alpera and La Minateda, with a great variety of subjects, epochs, styles and sizes. We find female figures, as at Cogull, warriors fighting and hunting as at Valltorta, a man climbing a rope as at Araña, and even deer and bulls that recall those of Albarracín. But besides these there are scenes full of originality, like a line of mountain goats, headed by the billy, with a very successfully achieved sense of movement.

WOMEN DANCING AROUND A MAN. EPIPALAEOLITHIC CAVE PAINTING OF EASTERN SPAIN. ABOUT 4000 B.C. SHELTER OF COGULL (LÉRIDA). AFTER MARTÍN ALMAGRO.

28

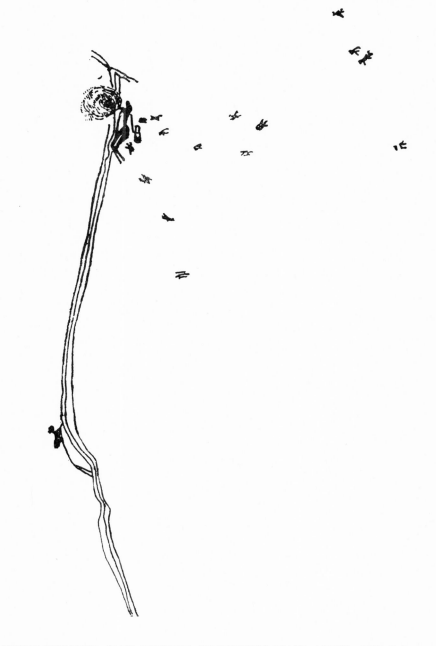

MAN COLLECTING HONEY. EPIPALAEOLITHIC CAVE PAINTING OF EASTERN SPAIN. ABOUT 4000 B.C.
CAVE OF ARAÑA, BICORP (VALENCIA). AFTER E. HERNÁNDEZ PACHECO.

The last phase of Spanish cave painting takes place in a period that is full of interest but raises exciting problems for Europe as a whole. What did the Neolithic Age mean in the Iberian peninsula? Did it arise as a result of the evolution of the peoples on the eastern coast, or as a result of the first European contacts with the far more advanced Mediterranean cultures? Probably it was the outcome of the changes brought about among the peoples of eastern Spain as a result of their contacts with the Middle East. There is no doubt that between the fourth and the first millennium B.C. countries like Mesopotamia and Egypt had a very advanced civilization; it is logical to consider the influence they must have had over more backward cultures. Among the Neolithic remains in Spain, the ceramics point to more refined ways of life. The megalithic dolmens, which have a funerary character, suggest much more spectacular monuments, like the pyramids, which were built for the same purpose.

The Neolithic or New Stone age was followed by the age of metals, and the two are closely linked; it is hard to divide the dolmen constructions and the early pottery forms from the oldest bronze objects that have been discovered. Thus perfect continuity can be established with the periods that stand on the threshold of history, at the beginning of what is called the Iron Age, when the first millennium B.C. begins.

Between the Neolithic and Bronze cultures comes the last period of cave painting, which in Spain is extremely interesting. From the naturalism of Altamira we pass on to forms in which the abstract is dominant. Starting from subjects that suggest a link with the artists of eastern Spain, Neolithic painters took an important step forward in the schematic treatment of their figures, which they reduced to pure ideograms. A human being can be represented by strokes indicating head, trunk and extremities; but certain parts of the body, even one as vital as the head, may be omitted altogether and a vertical stroke may indicate trunk and legs: thus an outline "T" comes to be a symbol with an anthropomorphic value. Similar processes of synthesis take place with the figures of animals. But no single, universally valid standard can explain this diagrammatic art. Each cave and shelter has its own solutions, but this does not prevent artistic connections being established: there are similarities in the use of color (various colors being employed, though there are usually monochrome figures as well), in the way the figures are schematized, in the rhythms of composition, and so on. Apart from this, there are, as in the earlier caves, paintings superimposed on others of different periods, which again suggest they may have had some magical purpose (the term religious still seems premature). The Neolithic paintings are thus already very close to the diagrams from which, in other Mediterranean cultures, the first forms of writing arose.

All this makes schematic art extraordinarily exciting: it shows how local elements (mainly those of eastern Spain) were crossed with others from the Middle East. The imported motifs might have come as decoration on ceramic wares and other objects, and the local people may have copied them on the rock walls. Some of the paintings have subjects which had already appeared in Mesopotamia, Anatolia, the Cyclades, Cyprus and Crete.

Schematic art extended over the whole of the Iberian peninsula. But its expansion appears the more logical in places where eastern cultures very obviously penetrated, near the Mediterranean seaboard, especially in the southeast; in the valley of the Guadalquivir and in the Tagus lowlands from Portugal to the plateau of Castile. In each region, of course, it developed its own special features, which varied according to

SCHEMATIC FIGURES. NEOLITHIC OR BRONZE AGE CAVE PAINTING. ABOUT 2000 B.C.
SHELTER OF LOS LETREROS, VÉLEZ BLANCO (ALMERÍA).

the strength of outside influences or of eastern Spanish traditions. Spain's connections with other peoples can, in fact, be followed through these cave paintings. Although it is impossible to date them exactly, it grows ever clearer that they are relatively close to our own time. Perhaps most of the known works belong to the third and second millenniums B.C.

An eloquent example of how schematism appears in cave painting is found in the shelter of Los Letreros, very near to Vélez Blanco (Almería). Human and animal figures, in some cases superimposed, are found there; living beings, which even look as if they are moving, can easily be recognized in the red or brown drawings, and some of them are grouped together. All the same, the abstract dominates them—human forms are reduced to triangles, and animals are synthesized by lines that suggest head, body and legs.

Cave painting thus developed from the naturalism of Altamira to the schematic art of its final stage. And today, three thousand years later, this evolution seems to anticipate the progress of modern art, from realism to abstraction.

THE PRESENCE OF THE MEDITERRANEAN WORLD

The evolution of cave painting has taken us through a period of nearly twenty thousand years. In the first millennium B.C. Spanish art is, quite unmistakably, already in close contact with that of other peoples, since the Iberian peninsula attracted sailors from the eastern Mediterranean. Spain's image was found even in the world of mythology. Gilgamesh, the Mesopotamian hero, is said to have journeyed to its shores; some of the labors of Hercules took place there; the garden of the Hesperides seems to have been there and it was near Cadiz that Geryon had his herd of cattle. The Pillars of Hercules, set up at the Straits of Gibraltar to celebrate the heroic deeds of the Greek hero, marked a boundary beyond which lay unknown seas. In the Greek world, Spain was a distant, legendary country, but as the centuries passed it also became a goal for seamen who traded busily with the peoples of the eastern Mediterranean.

Today there can be no doubt that the earliest settlers in various parts of Andalusia and the Balearic Islands came in search of metals. Here there was gold, silver and copper; tin, which was indispensable for making bronze, was plentiful beyond the Straits of Gibraltar in the islands of Cassiterides, which may have been on the coast of Galicia or of England—we still do not know which. Even today it is instructive to prove, archaeologically, the age of many of the metal mines around which cultural centers arose in the middle of the Bronze Age, during the second millennium B.C. Fruitful contacts between the native peoples and others from the eastern Mediterranean were thus possible.

Cretan ships may have reached the Balearic Islands during the second millennium. The highly original culture that developed in these islands shows curious contacts with pre-Hellenic culture. But many works with a distinctly eastern flavor are of a much later date. The best examples are found in some funerary monuments with simulated vaulting, and especially in some bulls' heads found in Majorca. In a settlement excavated at Costitx (Majorca) three magnificent bronze heads with several loose horns, also of bronze, were found; all were surprisingly realistic in feeling. Naturally these recall the cult of the bull and the value it had in the Minoan cultures, where it was constantly represented, sometimes in heads carved in the round that seem, in a remote way, to foreshadow our own animals. Unfortunately, archaeologists have found that Balearic art tends to be extremely archaic; indeed, the discoveries at Costitx may even belong within Roman times. All the same, from the bison of Altamira, through the mythological world, to the bulls of Majorca, the bull remains a symbol of Spain.

We know little about the presence of Cretan seamen in the West. But there is abundant archaeological and historical evidence that the Phoenicians or Carthaginians, coming

BRONZE BULL'S HEAD FROM COSTITX (MAJORCA). FIRST MILLENNIUM B.C.
NATIONAL ARCHAEOLOGICAL MUSEUM, MADRID.

originally from the coasts of Asia Minor, from Tyre and Sidon, settled in Cadiz, beyond the straits, towards the end of the second millennium. We know that these merchants founded a series of small towns along the Andalusian coast, like Malaca, Sexi and Abdera. The discoveries made in 1963 in a necropolis at Almuñécar (the ancient Sexi) brought to light alabaster vases with Egyptian "scrolls" from the eighth century B.C. These confirmed, without any doubt, that objects which influenced the art of the natives were imported.

Later came the earliest Greek settlers, who founded trading colonies in the south of Spain, such as the one at Mainake, in rivalry with the Phoenicians. In the naval battle of Alalia (537 B.C.) the Phoenicians established their supremacy (they were also firmly settled in Carthage), and thus Greek trade with southern Spain was interrupted. A second Greek colonization of the eastern coast, however, took place, especially in Catalonia: this time undertaken by the Greeks of Massalia (Marseilles). These people continued here until the coming of the Romans, so that a great many cultural remains of Greece and Rome have been found in one of their main cities, Ampurias, on the northern coast of Catalonia.

With what peoples were the Phoenician and Greek seamen in contact? In the first millennium B.C. we must link the people who lived in the peninsula with place-names that have some historical meaning. The oldest of these is Tartessos. Since, nearly fifty years ago, Professor Schulten began studying in depth what primitive Spain might mean, research has gone on in an effort to understand the enigma. The Bible keeps mentioning the ships of Tarshish, which in Solomon's time brought to Israel gold, silver and apes. Might these apes be the ancestors of those still surviving on the Rock of Gibraltar? There are extremely interesting references to Tartessos also in the *Ora Maritima* of Avienus, a description of the Mediterranean coast written about 400 A.D., but using information about a long voyage made by a Greek from Marseilles in the sixth century B.C. Many other ancient texts mention Tartessos.

Tartessos seems, in fact, to have been an important trading post with a solid political organization, the center of a great Andalusian culture. Some historians have suggested it stood between the mouth of the Guadalquivir (in Coto de Doñana, where there is an important sea-bird sanctuary) and the estuary of Huelva, and have identified it with Plato's Atlantis; and more recently the island of Saltés, hard by the place where Columbus's ships set sail, has been a more popular site for it. So far, unfortunately, it has proved impossible to say firmly, on the basis of excavations or ancient texts, where in fact Tartessos stood. With a stretch of the imagination one might consider it the first organized state in ancient Spain, extending across western Andalusia, and in close contact with the original Phoenicians and Greeks. The culture it created would be the highest achieved by the development of the Neolithic and Bronze Age peoples on the shores of the Mediterranean.

GOLD BRACELET FROM THE VILLENA
TREASURE. EARLY FIRST MILLENNIUM
B.C. VILLENA (ALICANTE).

But whether we like it or not, Tartessos remains a charming myth. In some cases, the artistic treasures of the first millennium B.C. are attributed to it, but it seems preferable to attribute them to others, the Iberians and the Celts, both of them vigorous peoples who formed the basis of pre-Roman Spain. Tradition says that the Iberians were related to ethnic groups from the Middle East, and for this reason their art drew a great deal from the Mediterranean peoples; whereas the Celts were connected with much poorer central European groups assimilated in the Hallstatt period, within the first Iron Age. The Iberians played a major role in ancient history, not just within the peninsula that bears their name, but as mercenaries to the Greeks and the Carthaginians; so they appear in the wars that took place between the sixth and third centuries B.C. in Sicily, Sardinia, the Peloponnese, southern Italy and North Africa. Very likely returning soldiers brought objects with them from the countries they had visited, thus helping to enrich the Mediterranean influences on Spanish art.

The studies made by Arribas have emphasized the geographical meaning that attaches to the word "Iberian" in classical texts. Often it includes peoples of varying cultures at very disparate times. This accounts for the varied aspects of Iberian art. Its oldest works (sixth and fifth centuries) show links with Phoenician and Greek art; indeed they have been called "Tartessio-Iberian." But the later works show the influence of the Roman world, for by this time we are almost at the beginning of the Christian era.

Celtic art, which also developed very unevenly, appears mainly in the north and center of the peninsula, but in some cases its influence reached as far as Andalusia. Where the two overlap (in particular in Castile), it becomes Celtic-Iberian art. So in the interior of the country and the Cantabrian watershed we find works with the most varied tendencies, not simply Central European and Greco-Punic, but in some cases Italic, which means there are even strange links with Etruscan art. Works of Celtic origin are, with a few exceptions, greatly inferior to Iberian works, and there is no doubt at all that in ancient Spain the Mediterranean cultures were the more important.

Abundant gold jewelry from the second millennium B.C. has been found, much of it in this century; the last few years in particular have seen important discoveries. The most recent finds were made in Seville (El Carambolo, 1959) and Villena (Alicante, 1963).

GOLD PENDANT
FROM THE ALISEDA TREASURE
(CÁCERES). 6TH-5TH CENTURY B.C.
NATIONAL ARCHAEOLOGICAL
MUSEUM, MADRID.

BRONZE LAMPSTAND FROM CALACEITE (TERUEL), DETAIL. NATIONAL ARCHAEOLOGICAL MUSEUM, MADRID.

composition of its frieze appears in works of a very different kind and ancestry: it even recalls the archaic Greek ceramics of the Dipylon. Other details, like the cones, suggest Carthaginian motifs, which may have been known through Iberian art. In fact, quite clearly this jewel made by the Celts in Galicia had a great variety of elements in it.

Other treasures take us completely into the field of Mediterranean art, although occasionally elements appear in them that have a Nordic ancestry. A recent discovery made in Villena is useful in dating the jewelry. It consists of sixty-seven objects—bowls, bottles, armlets and clasps, nearly all of them gold. An armlet stands out from the rest: five hoops can be distinguished, with mouldings decorated with spikes. It is surprising that the nearest parallel to this armlet is found in a similar piece of jewelry discovered almost a century ago in Estremoz (Portugal). The latter seems to be of Hallstatt origin and shows clearly how foreign works were copied and adapted within the Peninsula. What is remarkable is to find motifs of Nordic origin in the eastern part of Spain, in a collection that, for other reasons, was linked with Mediterranean cultures during the Bronze Age. The Villena treasure can therefore be dated to the beginning of the first millennium B.C.

The Carambolo treasure, found four years before that of Villena, in 1959, is another spectacular collection. There are only twenty-one objects in it, but the gold is of high quality (24 carat) and weighs over six pounds altogether. It includes a magnificent necklace, armlets, breastplates and other adornments. In all of them the decoration is extremely rich, although a little monotonous and repetitive at times, with a great many alternating spheres and rosettes. The style shows obvious links with the eastern Mediterranean, and similar objects have been found in Cyprus and Samos; but a few details suggest connections with the Etruscan world. The Carambolo treasure can be dated to the sixth century B.C.

Other pieces of jewelry show influences that are exclusively Greek: the Diadem of Jávea, for instance, and the earrings of Santiago de la Espada. One of these earrings is beautifully made, and as many as six independent elements can be seen in it. The main one is almost round, and about two inches in diameter; in this tiny space various decorative motifs appear, among them rosettes, spirals, S-shaped designs, and half-spheres with a rough surface. Another shows a small winged female figure, with a goblet in its right hand and a dove in its left. Relief is achieved by strips of embossed gold soldered along the edges. Similarities with other jewelry found in various parts of Greece mean that the Santiago de la Espada earrings can be dated between the fifth and fourth centuries B.C.

These, and a great deal more jewelry, show how important ornaments were in primitive Spain. But the art of metal work developed in other fields too, which complement the work of the jewellers. Two objects are particularly significant. One, from Calaceite, is

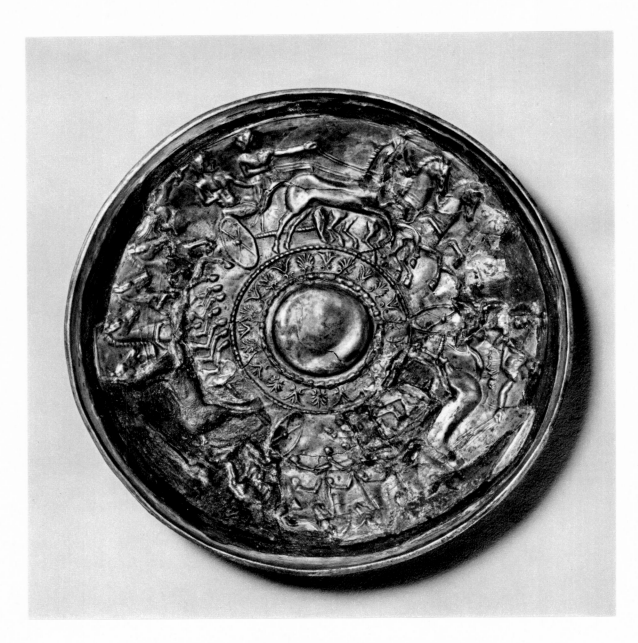

SILVER PATEN FROM TIVISA (TARRAGONA). ABOUT 4TH CENTURY B.C.
ARCHAEOLOGICAL MUSEUM, BARCELONA.

now in the National Archaeological Museum in Madrid; it is said to be a bronze lamp-stand and is a strange object with a circular base and a stem in the middle with a horse attached to it; a platform, also circular, stands on top of the stem and must have held a lamp. The decoration is very simple: a series of cylindrical motifs, sometimes twisted into the form of a rope. The rope motif is typically Celtic and the small slender horse seems to suggest Hallstatt works, but it recalls similar archaic Greek objects as well.

The lampstand of Calaceite, which was found in a tomb, is from the point of view of style much like the Diadem of Ribadeo. But in the second of the two important objects —the paten of Tivisa—completely Mediterranean influences dominate. The paten,

PAINTED IBERIAN VASE FROM THE NECROPOLIS OF VERDOLAY (MURCIA). 5TH-4TH CENTURY B.C.
ARCHAEOLOGICAL MUSEUM, MURCIA.

which is probably the finest piece of silver-work found in the Peninsula, was discovered with another, simpler one in Tarragona, and its similarity to others found in the south of France has suggested that it may have been made in a workshop set up in the western Mediterranean (in Provence or Catalonia), but which imitated Greek models of about the fourth century B.C. On the silver background are classical palmettes, from which three chariots, each carrying two people, unfold in a circle. The effect of depth, and of movement in the horses, is masterly.

Connections with the cultures of the eastern Mediterranean appear very clearly in the field of ceramics; from the Neolithic Age onwards, and increasingly in the Iberian period. There are any number of possible examples, among them the extremely delicate vases from the necropolis of Verdolay (Murcia), in which motifs of obviously Greek origin are combined with ornamental forms created, no doubt, by the potters of south-eastern Spain about the fifth and fourth century B.C.

Then there is sculpture. In a necropolis at Galera (Granada), in a district of great archaeological interest, a small alabaster figure, with undoubtedly Egyptian antecedents, was discovered: a seated woman with sphinxes on either side. This may possibly represent a Phoenician goddess, Astarte, who here is a symbol of fertility.

The ornamentation of this small statue lies mainly in the clothes, whereas in other, much coarser, Carthaginian objects what counts most is the jewels and other external elements. In spite of its extreme crudity the so-called Lady of Ibiza, found in a necropolis on the island, is well worth illustrating, because its background is classical, and because, although the face shows traces of the Greek tendency to idealize, an effort has been made to make the features definite and personal. The two necklaces and the hair ornaments show how jewels were used during the first millennium B.C.—and even abused.

To the Iberian, not Phoenician, artistic world belongs the statuette known as the Lady of Elche, a work of high quality. It takes its name from the town near Alicante where it was found in 1897. At the time it was suggested that this bejewelled woman was some "dark queen," and certainly it appears an exotic, eastern-looking figure. Its Orientalism, though, in no way resembles the Mohammedan air that came many centuries later, but is the kind brought to the Peninsula by the seamen who roamed the Mediterranean in ancient times.

The Lady of Elche is made of soft white limestone. The bust stands over 20 inches high and is part of a full-length statue. It may represent a priestess with offerings, in an attitude similar to that which appears in the complete figure found in the Cerro de los Santos in the province of Albacete. Originally, it must have been entirely colored; there are still plentiful traces of color on the lips and in the diadem round the brow.

ALABASTER STATUETTE OF THE GODDESS ASTARTE (?) FROM THE NECROPOLIS OF GALERA (GRANADA). 4TH-3RD CENTURY B.C. NATIONAL ARCHAEOLOGICAL MUSEUM, MADRID.

THE LADY OF IBIZA. TERRACOTTA. 4TH CENTURY B.C. NATIONAL ARCHAEOLOGICAL MUSEUM, MADRID.

A careful study of the face reveals how the sculptor tried to make it as correct as possible, and at the same time kept certain features that made it individual—indeed, to some extent a portrait. This realistic effect is enhanced by the eyes, in which the iris is sunken: this must have been covered with some paste. The expression is severe, without being hieratic. The sides of the face, only slightly modelled, and the very thick neck give it character.

The ornaments worn by the Lady of Elche are very important. Several necklaces, decorated with tiny amphorae, lie on the breast. The face is surrounded by two large hoops, which must surely show where some gold ornament once appeared, to bind the hair. From the inner part of these hoops hang pendants, ending in small amphorae. The diadem that covers the hair is decorated with spheres. The Lady wears a tunic and a cloak covers her shoulders and hangs down in zigzag folds. At the back of the figure there is a cavity: what this means is not clear, but it probably had some religious function; perhaps offerings were deposited in it.

What place does this beautiful figure occupy in the history of Spanish art? It is undoubtedly the first piece of sculpture of high quality found in the Peninsula, which nobly expresses the characteristics of a specifically Iberian style. Its ornaments are artistically similar to the jewels we have described. Perhaps it would not have been achieved without the influence of the Greek world; yet in spite of all the influences on it the Lady of Elche shows for the first time an art already imbued with national feeling.

BRONZE HEAD OF THE EMPEROR AUGUSTUS (?) FROM AZAILA (TERUEL). FIRST CENTURY B.C. NATIONAL ARCHAEOLOGICAL MUSEUM, MADRID.

INCORPORATION IN THE ROMAN WORLD

Works of art found in Spain during the Bronze and Iron Ages, that is, during the first millennium B.C., are the result of a complex series of contacts with other peoples, mainly those of the Mediterranean world. The Phoenician and Greek seamen brought products of many different countries to the Catalonian and Andalusian seaboard, which gave what was basically a miscellaneous character to many works produced. The importance of decoration and the ornamental motifs employed show that an Oriental concept of art predominated. But gradually, and in particular from the middle of the fifth century B.C., the classical spirit began to be felt by way of the Greek colonies, which played an extremely important role in Spanish art: through them must have come sculpture, pottery, metal objects and other imported works that influenced it profoundly.

Concentrating merely on the findings at Ampurias, on the coast of Catalonia, the only Greek city in Spain that has been excavated systematically, it is possible to see the reflection of Greek styles from the age of Pericles until after the death of Alexander the Great. We have already noted some typically Hellenic objects, like the paten of Tivisa. In Ampurias sculptures like the magnificent head of Aphrodite, which recalls Praxiteles, and the statue of Aesculapius, from the Hellenistic age, helped to forward the triumph of classicism.

A series of historical events upset the continuity of this development, however. The invasion of the Carthaginians (Phoenicians established at Carthage), who founded the city of Cartagena in southeastern Spain and spread out from there, had important results. Owing to the presence of the Carthaginians, Spain was involved in the Punic Wars, and in order to halt Hannibal's march on Italy the Romans landed in the Peninsula in 218 B.C. This began a wholly new stage in Spanish history. When Rome triumphed over Carthage, a century's fighting followed before the whole of the Iberian territory was occupied by the Romans. The Lusitanian, Numantian and Cantabrian wars lasted from the beginning of the second century B.C. until the time of Augustus. Inland, the fighting was bitter and the natives, often organized as guerilla fighters, gave the Romans an excessive amount of trouble. Today, however much we may admire their heroism and however moving the tragic sacrifice of the city of Numantia may seem, we are bound to welcome the fact that Rome eventually triumphed. Thanks to this, Spain was integrated in the classical world.

The whole of the Iberian peninsula was romanized: the process started along the shores of the Mediterranean but it soon spread inland and into the remotest corners of Spain. Roads were built linking cities like Tarragona, Saragossa, León, Astorga, Salamanca,

THE ROMAN BRIDGE OF ALCÁNTARA (CÁCERES). 105-106 A.D.

Mérida and Seville, and great cities arose in which Roman civilization was definitely established. Thus the chances of a native Iberian art arising, which works like the Lady of Elche had seemed so forcefully to suggest, were frustrated. For Rome was a great leveller. All the countries incorporated in the Roman Empire very quickly assimilated its art, which seemed to sterilize their native efforts.

The most fertile stage of romanization was from the age of Augustus (27 B.C.-14 A.D.) to that of Trajan (98-117 A.D.). Having ceased to rebel, Spain contributed to the expansion of the Empire in the political field, as much as in the cultural. In the first century A.D., what meagre virtues Nero's government had were owed to a Stoic philosopher, Seneca, who was born in Cordova, then one of the leading Hispano-Roman cities. In the same era, the great Roman poet Martial was also a Spaniard. Trajan, the greatest emperor after Augustus, was born in Seville, and Theodosius was also born in the Iberian peninsula. These and others prove fully how Spain was incorporated in the Roman world.

As happened in other countries of the Empire, the works of art this age produced in Spain, though provincial, were outstanding. Bridges that, because of their high quality and strength, are still in use, were built to complement the magnificent network of roads: none, in the whole of the Roman world, is finer than the bridge at Alcántara.

It crosses the river Tagus, its six arches spanning a deep gorge. In order to keep level with the road two arches nearly 100 feet across and 157 feet high were built, all in square-hewn granite stones that emphasized the solidity and monumentality of the structure. The bridge is on the road into Portugal from Cáceres. Fortunately it is dated, thanks to an inscription to Trajan that gives us the year as 105-106 A.D. We know, besides, that it was built from contributions made by a number of Lusitanian towns. On the central pillar stands an arch of triumph and at one end a simple shrine. Though it has been somewhat restored, it is admirably preserved.

This, and many other bridges (one at Mérida, for instance, which is half a mile long, and those at Salamanca and Alconétar), show only one aspect of the importance of public works in Roman Spain. The aqueducts that survive are in some cases unique of their kind. This is so, for instance, at Segovia, where the aqueduct, over 2300 feet long and with two tiers of arches that raise it to a height of 100 feet, is the finest and best preserved in the whole Roman Empire. Those at Tarragona and Mérida are also interesting; in Mérida, the aqueduct of Los Milagros, made of stone and brick, is especially valuable because it shows techniques that were later put to good use in the Great Mosque of Cordova.

Spanish architecture flourished in Roman times, and much of it survives. Towns such as León, Tarragona, and Barcelona retain a large part of their Roman walls; Lugo, in Galicia, is still completely surrounded by them. At Medinaceli (Soria), Bará (Tarragona), Capera (Cáceres) and Mérida there are still triumphal arches. After a great deal of excavation and restoration, the Roman theater at Mérida stands high among those that are still preserved. Amphitheaters, baths, temples, mausoleums, and houses all testify to the importance of romanization in Spain.

A great deal of sculpture of the period has been discovered during these excavations. Everywhere, but particularly at Tarragona, Mérida and Itálica (Seville), many statues, busts and sarcophagi have come to light, and they raise complex problems—for instance, when it is a matter of deciding which were imported and which were made in the Peninsula. But although provincial features can be found in many of these sculptural works, neither their quality nor their stylistic contacts with the art of the Empire can be denied. One example among many shows this: a bronze head probably representing Augustus when he was thirty-one, discovered at Azaila (Teruel). It is the oldest portrait of the emperor preserved in the Peninsula and recalls the effigy of him after the triumph at Actium. It is a serene-looking work, and perhaps the Spanish artist wanted to accentuate the features that expressed Augustus's individuality.

Many important pagan and Early Christian sarcophagi have been found in Spain, and they show how the art of relief developed in the Roman world during the early centuries of the Christian era. Some are of high quality, in particular the sarcophagus

FRONT OF A MARBLE SARCOPHAGUS FOUND AT CORDOVA. EARLY 3RD CENTURY A.D. ALCAZAR OF THE CHRISTIAN KINGS, CORDOVA.

found at Cordova in 1958, which in its center shows the door of Hades, the kingdom of the dead, half-open, with two figures on each side of it. These figures are of a man and a woman about to enter the world of shades, each guided by another of the same sex. Other allegorical representations of death are the figures of Pegasus on the ends of the sarcophagus. This splendid work, with all its symbols, is quite exceptional in Spanish art; it was made at the beginning of the third century A.D., and the exaggeration of certain details (particularly the twisted columns and the flecked draperies) does not detract from the calm melancholy of the figures. Quite possibly it was imported from Rome, where today another work similar to it is preserved in the Vatican.

A sarcophagus found ten years earlier in the sea, near the shore at Tarragona, is composed in a more complex way. Its four sides are carved and tell the story of the ill-fated Hippolytus, son of Theseus, who was trampled to death by his chariot horses, which were frightened by one of Poseidon's bulls. The scene of the tragedy is carved in low relief on the back of the sarcophagus, which contrasts with the front side, with almost unobstructed figures. The composition, which is roughly sketched in, has immense plastic energy: the contrast between the horses, rearing up on their hind legs, and the figure of Hippolytus lying on his back, Theseus's expression of suffering as he tears at his beard, these and other details give it remarkable beauty. This work is unique of its kind in the Peninsula and was probably brought from Rome, inspired by a Greek model of the Hellenistic age, though made in the second or third century A.D.

These examples sufficiently indicate the quality and significance of the works imported into Spain. It is logical that the best works came from Rome, and excelled the provincial local products. The Disk of Theodosius, found over a century ago in Estremadura and now in the Academy of History in Madrid, is another example; a masterpiece of its kind, beautifully made and measuring 29 inches in diameter. Thanks to its inscription we know its exact date: January 19, 388. The disk is of silver and appears to have been gilt and embossed. It shows, under an archway, the seated figures of the Emperor (who is in the center), Valentinian II and Arcadius. In the corners are pairs of soldiers with bucklers and in the lower part a large reclining figure, with two allegorical putti. The Disk of Theodosius closes a great chapter in the history of Spanish art. It must have been made in the Greek east, but was surely made to be sent to the far west of the Empire. Thus, when Spain was closely linked with the classical world as represented by Rome, timid hints of Orientalism were appearing. With Theodosius, a Spanish emperor, the Empire's life and art were turning eastward. It was in that very year, 388, that the emperor was in Constantinople.

BACK OF THE MARBLE SARCOPHAGUS OF HIPPOLYTUS. 2ND-3RD CENTURY A.D. TARRAGONA MUSEUM.

SILVER DISK OF THEODOSIUS. DATED 388 A.D. ROYAL ACADEMY OF HISTORY, MADRID.

It was thus that Spain crossed the threshold of art. What happened from Altamira until Roman times was decisive for its future. When the Roman Empire fell, Spain was an historical reality with close, centuries-old contacts with other cultures. It was then that a synthesis was achieved. When the Middle Ages began, the men who by then had a right to call themselves Spaniards had a wide range of ancestors: those who made the cave paintings, those who lived in Tartessos, those who landed on the east coast and the shores of Andalusia in Greek and Phoenician ships, the Celtic tribes and the Iberian settlements, those who came from Carthage and founded Cartagena, and the Roman legionaries who stayed on as settlers.

Sánchez Albornoz believed, with good reason, that this complex country that was given the name of Spain was essentially born of the Roman Hispania. By the time the Germanic tribes invaded the country, the people of Spain were more strongly united than ever. But a new age of conflict began with the coming of the Goths and, three centuries later, that of the Moors. For a thousand years the Peninsula was to be strung between East and West, as mediator between the two or as the transmitter of the cultures that met and crossed there, and have left their mark on Spanish history and Spanish art.

THE TRIUMPH OF
THE EAST IN THE WEST

THE GREAT MOSQUE OF CORDOVA: ENTRANCE OF THE MIHRAB (PRAYER RECESS). 965-968.

In ancient times Spain profited by its fertile contact with the various cultures that developed around the Mediterranean. In these cultures a conflict of values was already discernible, a fundamental opposition between their ways of looking at life and art. The terms East and West took on a profound meaning. Face to face, they symbolized a tension that at critical times snapped. But this conflict still allowed periods of mutual understanding. The classical art of the ancient world could not have existed without the heritage of the East, which in turn benefited from the contributions of the West.

When the Roman Empire split into two and, after the reign of Theodosius (379-395 A.D.), Byzantium arose as an independent entity, art entered a period of acute crisis. Constantinople was a cultural center that absorbed the artistic traditions of the entire Middle East; but it also assimilated the great architectural advances of Rome. It was thus that at one end of the Mediterranean an extremely interesting artistic period began, which was to extend across the entire Middle Ages, and even beyond.

At the other end of the Mediterranean was Spain, which for centuries had been a part of the Roman world. At the time of the Germanic invasions, something happened that was to have an enormous effect upon the future of Spanish art. On the one hand, when Rome ceased to be the great unifier, when contact was broken between the various parts of the Empire, some native traditions were revived; in some buildings we find ornamental motifs which existed before the Roman conquest and had continued to figure in works of a popular kind. These native elements were mixed with others brought in by the barbarians. The Suevi, the Vandals, and above all the Visigoths, reveal themselves in the characteristic style of their minor arts; these nomadic peoples, who were seeking to settle down within the borders of the Empire, used a great deal of jewelry and other adornments, which were easy to carry. Another factor is that eastern Spain was occupied in the sixth century by the Byzantines, who intervened in the struggle for power within the unstable Visigothic kingdom. So, once again, the Iberian peninsula became a great artistic center where various currents converged.

Several parallel tendencies can accordingly be traced through Spanish art in the period from the fifth to the eighth century. Basically, what counted was the Roman tradition, especially in architecture. But in decoration indigenous and Germanic influences were dominant. Then there was the Byzantine influence as well, which of course added a strain of Orientalism to the native and Germanic styles of decoration. For three centuries, while the influence of classical ideals was diminishing, an unsettled situation favored the ascendancy of the East.

This brings us to a critical year: 711, in which a handful of Arabs with North African troops crossed the Straits of Gibraltar and invaded the Peninsula. These Moslem forces met scarcely any resistance. The Visigothic rulers were powerless against the fanatical invaders, and at the battle of Guadalete the last Gothic king, Roderick, was killed. The conquest of the whole of Spain was helped by the Jewish communities and by the indifference of the romanized Spaniards who, being subject to the barbarians, were merely changing masters. Invincibly, the Moslems advanced and crossed the Pyrenees. In France they were finally halted by Charles Martel at the battle of Poitiers (732). Many historians consider that the Moslem invasion in 711 marks Spain's real entry into the Middle Ages, which ended when the Christians reconquered Granada in 1492. For nearly eight centuries Arab civilization was to have one of its main centers at the furthest western point of the Mediterranean; at some periods in its development it reached a higher level than any of the surrounding Christian peoples of the West. This must be borne in mind if we are to understand the vital importance of Spain at certain times in the Middle Ages. The Moslems were the great sifters and transmitters of cultural forms, not merely those of eastern origin, but those of classical antiquity as well. No other people so thoroughly assimilated what they found in conquered countries, and from this blend of cultures the Iberian peninsula was to benefit.

Moslem rule in Spain falls into four distinct periods: (1) that of the Caliphate of Cordova, from the eighth to the tenth century; (2) that of the small kingdoms known as Taifas, during the eleventh century; (3) that of the Almohads in the twelfth century; (4) and during the thirteenth, fourteenth and fifteenth centuries, the age of the Nasrid kingdom of Granada.

Under the caliphs Cordova became a great city where science, literature, poetry and the arts flourished with unusual brilliance. The Christian kings came to the Andalusian capital to seek medical care, and many others came from all over Europe for cultural reasons. The various religions coexisted there: living side by side with the Moslems, both Christians and Jews were allowed to keep their own customs and laws.

Shortly after the year 1000 the Caliphate came to an end. When Al-Mansur died, things moved to a crisis and Moorish Spain was broken up into a score of petty kingdoms, called Taifas, ruled by the governors of the leading Moslem cities from

Andalusia to Saragossa. This situation of course favored the Christian kings, who had been gathering in the north of the Peninsula and were advancing southwards. The courts of these minor Taifa kings were very brilliant, all the same; they made up for their lack of political power by emphasizing the outward signs of it. Great fortified strongholds were built, with magnificent palaces, and there are still remnants of this fleeting splendor in Saragossa, Málaga, and Almería.

The factional strife of the Taifa kingdoms brought a number of invasions from North African peoples, who helped to contain the Christians' advance. The Almoravids, who came in the middle of the eleventh century, left almost no trace in art. But the Almohads, who made Seville into a great capital, seemed to be emulating the glories of Cordova when they built the great mosque (of which the famous Giralda tower and the Court of Oranges have survived) and the Alcazar. The conquest of the valley of the Guadalquivir by Castilian troops in the thirteenth century ended the Almohad empire in Spain.

The last stage of Islamic culture in Spain is to be seen in Granada. Dominating eastern Andalusia, protected by a range of mountains, but with outlets to the sea from Málaga to Almería, the Nasrid kingdom of Granada developed between the thirteenth and fifteenth centuries, with periods of great power. This last center of Orientalism had enduring effects on the subsequent history of Spain, and specifically in the field of art. Influenced as it was by distant Middle Eastern countries, Granada in its turn had a profound influence upon the Christians, both before and after it was conquered by them.

This brief survey of the Islamic period is enough to explain how the East penetrated the West through Spain in the Middle Ages. But in this artistic exchange, an important part was played by the Mozarabs, Mudejars and Moriscos. The Christians—known as Mozarabs—who had stayed in Moorish Spain, keeping their own religion, laws and customs (which the invaders respected in exchange for a high tribute), began to emigrate towards the reconquered territories in the northern half of the country. During the tenth century, from Galicia to Catalonia and through Castile, an art arose in which Moslem and Christian elements were mingled and fused. Without this Mozarab current, styles like the Romanesque cannot be explained.

As Spain was gradually reconquered by the Christians, something happened that can be interpreted in quite the opposite way. In the reconquered cities, such as Toledo (1085), Saragossa (1118), Cordova (1236) and Seville (1248), large groups of Moslems remained—known as Mudejars—whose art was vitally important, especially in the thirteenth and fourteenth centuries. When they became Christians, they were called Moriscos; but this hardly affected the art forms they used, which even after the close of the Middle Ages remained distinctively Oriental.

VISIGOTHIC CHURCH OF SAN PEDRO DE LA NAVE (ZAMORA): VIEW OF THE INTERIOR. 7TH-8TH CENTURY (?).

TEMPLES OF THREE RELIGIONS

The coexistence of Moslems, Christians and Jews in medieval Spain had important effects in the field of art. Although their forms of worship were very different, in architecture and decoration there were certain links between them; and these show where Oriental features began, and how they were maintained. A great deal was brought in from the eastern-facing world of Islam, and fused with what had a totally different origin. Some elements are constant, and give character and unity to works that are very far apart in space and time.

The first traces of Orientalism appear in the Visigothic churches, which show the influence of Byzantine art. The presence of the horseshoe arch in them raises an interesting question: did it derive from the Hispano-Roman tomb reliefs on which it figures, or from the early Christian churches of Syria? This uncertainty is typical of the problems that keep arising in any analysis of the conflict between East and West in the Iberian peninsula.

Another aspect of the problem can be seen in the decoration of Visigothic churches. In two of them, Quintanilla de las Viñas and San Pedro de la Nave, whose date is unknown (Camón Aznar considers them to be of the eighth century), the decoration recalls that of certain ivory carvings from Asia Minor and Ravenna. In Visigothic capitals there is a definite Byzantinism in the form (the trunk of an inverted pyramid) and in the development of the ogee, which departs from the traditional module of classical art.

The Visigothic horseshoe arch was taken up and widely used in Spain. For many centuries it is to be found in mosques, churches and synagogues. The most famous example is the Great Mosque of Cordova. When Abderrahman I (731-788, a member of the Omayyad family who was able to flee from Damascus when the Caliphate fell) reached Cordova in 756 and there founded an emirate independent of Baghdad, he decided to build a place of worship. He purchased the site of the Visigothic church of San Vicente and authorized the Christians to build another outside the city walls. What artistic relationship with the Christian church it supplanted this first mosque may have had, we do not know; most likely many disparate influences were fused in it. There are reminiscences of both classical and Visigothic architecture; but also of the Great Mosque of Damascus, which Abderrahman had admired from childhood.

In the mosque of Cordova we have a type of building that was completely new to Spain. It was not, strictly speaking, the house of God, but a place of collective prayer. The chief problem was that of finding enough room for the faithful. The structural

DANIEL IN THE LIONS' DEN. CAPITAL IN THE TRANSEPT OF THE VISIGOTHIC CHURCH
OF SAN PEDRO DE LA NAVE (ZAMORA). 7TH-8TH CENTURY (?).

system was such—a large hall, its roof supported by rows of columns forming a
series of aisles—that the mosque could be lengthened or widened as often as the need
arose, simply by adding more aisles, which were all of the same height. The aisles led
to the wall of the *qibla* (i.e. the direction of prayer); here was the prayer niche, the
mihrab, where the faithful came for their devotions. Usually the *mihrab* pointed in the
direction of Mecca, but in Cordova, for unknown reasons, it faced south. A courtyard,
with a basin of water for ablutions, and the minaret, the tower up which the muezzin
climbs to call the faithful to prayer, completed the mosque.

Abderrahman I built this, the first mosque in Spain, in a very short time. The documents mention only a single year (786), but very likely this was just the date at which

he purchased and took over the church of San Vicente. The plan of the new building was almost square. The part that was roofed, and had eleven aisles, was in the form of a rectangle, the larger sides being double the length of the smaller. As the walled courtyard was about the same size as the part under cover, the outer perimeter of the mosque had sides that were roughly equal, some 250 feet long. The outer walls, reinforced with buttresses, resembled those of the mosque in Damascus; but in Cordova the aisles were not parallel with the *qibla* wall, but perpendicular to it.

The original mosque of Abderrahman I was altered and enlarged at various times. The most extensive alterations were made by Abderrahman II (between 833 and 848), by Al-Hakam II (962-968) and Al-Mansur (987-c. 997). The first two caliphs lengthened the aisles, the third increased their number laterally, thus making an enormous rectangular building, covering an area of over three acres.

Abderrahman II extended the mosque by breaking through the *qibla* wall and adding seven bays. Like those who came after him, he preserved the original structure, so that the building never lost its unity. The most surprising additions are some Corinthian-type capitals that do not copy, but freely interpret, the classical models. Mohammed I and Abderrahman III made important additions during the ninth and tenth centuries, such as the door of San Esteban and the new minaret. But these are all less interesting than those of Al-Hakam II.

Keeping the eleven aisles, Al-Hakam took down the *qibla* wall again and prolonged the aisles by the addition of twelve bays, thus bringing the total length of the mosque to 525 feet. He introduced a number of elements, never seen before, which accentuated the Oriental style of the building. In his addition, the same system of roofs and columns was maintained, with slight variations, but it was enriched by the construction of four cupolas (one where his addition began and three close to the *mihrab*), which introduced a great many new features. Among these was a series of intersecting cusped arches, producing a beautiful ornamental effect and forming at the same time a supporting structure of great strength and lightness. The cupolas took the form of ribbed domes. The ribs, however, do not meet in the center of the dome, but criss-cross in the vaulting around the center—a new and original technique both structurally sound and highly decorative. These ribbed domes at Cordova can be considered the oldest surviving examples of their kind, though they may have been inspired by eastern prototypes we know nothing about. They in their turn are the most obvious forerunners we know of the typically Gothic ogive. This name, which may be derived from *aljibe* (cistern, water-tank), and the very unusual arrangement of the Moorish vaulting ribs, makes one wonder whether such ribbed domes may not have been used originally to cover water-tanks; if, when they were first made, they had a wooden shell on the outside, this would explain the space left open in the center through which the water must have been drawn.

SYNAGOGUE OF SANTA MARIA LA BLANCA, TOLEDO: VIEW OF THE INTERIOR. 13TH CENTURY.

The Great Mosque of Cordova, the church of San Miguel de Escalada (León), and the synagogue of Santa María la Blanca in Toledo all have horseshoe arches: they symbolize the connections that existed, over and above religious differences, between the various regions of medieval Spain. In the mosque at Cordova, the two tiers of arches, one above the other, recall those of Roman aqueducts, and channels to collect the water also run along the top of these arcades. The arches are supported not by stout pillars, however, but by slender columns. The voussoirs are made alternately of stone and brick, which gives beautiful polychromatic effects, and the use of materials of different density has the added effect of making the arches look lighter than they really are: aesthetic and structural values thus go together. When the mosque was converted into a Christian church in the sixteenth century, a cathedral was built in the center of it. This is the kind of thing that keeps happening in Spanish art: the great buildings tend to reflect the changing tastes of each generation, which is not content to accept them as they have come down from the past.

The Mozarabic church of San Miguel de Escalada (913), some 20 miles east of León, combines Christian and Moorish influences. It is a three-aisled basilica with three juxta-posed chapels at the east end and an entrance porch, its design reflecting Visigothic traditions as revived and handed down by Asturian churches of the ninth century. On the other hand, the horseshoe arches (which are suggested also in the layout of the chapels), the modillions supporting the eaves, and the sculptured capitals are all derived from the Moorish art of Cordova.

The synagogues of Santa María la Blanca and El Tránsito in Toledo, built during the thirteenth and fourteenth centuries, show Moorish influence both in their architecture and their decoration. Santa María la Blanca, with its five aisles and horseshoe arches, has the same multiplicity of supporting columns as the mosques. The sculptured capitals are decorated with fanciful pine-cones, and the spandrels between the arches with highly original tracery reliefs.

The art of Al-Hakam II's reign was in many ways original. We may note in the mosque such features as the stylized Corinthian capitals, the use of columns of different colors, and the greater richness of the central aisle between the domes. Most remarkable of all, from the decorative point of view, is the *mihrab*. Both the horseshoe arch at the entrance and the inner recess are panelled with marble and lavishly decorated with mosaics, the work of Byzantine artists. In these decorations we find a curious upsurge of Orientalism for which, in this case, Christian influence was responsible. The contacts between the Byzantine Empire and the Caliphate of Cordova show that sometimes religious and political barriers matter very little. In comparison with what Al-Hakam II achieved, Al-Mansur's work is of interest only from the spatial point of view: he added eight more aisles and enlarged the courtyard proportionately, bringing the mosque to its present size.

In 1002 Al-Mansur died and Moorish Spain was broken up into the small kingdoms called Taifas. Political weakness was hidden under ostentatious buildings that gave a false sense of richness. The solid architectural structure of the Great Mosque of Cordova gave way to forms that were purely ornamental. A few small chapels that have survived from this period give us a faint idea of what other places of worship must have been like.

The Almohad empire, which reached its height in the twelfth century, made Seville into a flourishing capital. There, near the Alcazar, one of the largest mosques of the Islamic west was built. In size it rivalled the mosque of Cordova, but its brick structure was nearer to that of North African buildings, such as the Kutubiya of Marrakesh. Its seventeen aisles were divided by brick pillars and pointed horseshoe arches. When the mosque of Seville was destroyed in the fifteenth century, to make way for the great Gothic cathedral, the builders had the happy idea of keeping the courtyard and the tower. With the belfry added in the sixteenth century, the Giralda is probably the most beautiful of all the Moorish towers in Spain and North Africa. The decoration is in perfect harmony with its solid structure. The cusped and horseshoe arches character-istic of the architecture of the Caliphate are here combined with pointed arches. Along the upper sides are vertical panels of brickwork forming patterns of lozenges. A frieze of blind arches completes the tower, at a height of 165 feet. Thus Moorish art main-tained its vitality, spreading such ideas as the pointed horseshoe arch, which were to extend to many other places in Spain. The Visigothic horseshoe arch, taken over by the Moslems, reappears in Christian Spain, brought from Andalusia by the Mozarabs.

When they went north, at the end of the ninth and throughout the tenth century, the Mozarabs, though wishing to make contact with the artistic ideas of the West, were still entranced by the glories of Cordova. So the churches they built in Galicia, León, Castile and Catalonia show a synthesis between Moorish architectural forms (with arches, vaults, and decorative motifs of the Caliphate period) and Christian forms.

HUNTING SCENE. WALL PAINTING FROM THE CHURCH OF SAN BAUDEL DE BERLANGA (SORIA). IOTH-IITH CENTURY. PRADO, MADRID.

The Mozarabs showed great versatility in the structural design of their churches, as if they were seeking to emphasize the difference between a church and a mosque. What they have in common is found in ornamental or constructional motifs, not in the way in which space is used. The variety of the Mozarabic churches can be explained only by their creative vigor: some have three aisles, some two, and others only one; sometimes they are made with fine materials, especially with stout, square-hewn stones, sometimes more modestly.

There are scarcely fifty Mozarabic buildings left in Spain, but these are excitingly varied. The Oriental aspect of their ornamentation is seen in the few pieces of sculpture and the wall paintings that have come down to us, with exceptional good fortune, in San Baudel de Berlanga (province of Soria). This is a very strange church, small and almost square (28 by 24½ feet), and yet architecturally it is complex, and planned, apparently, to avoid using wood. In the center stands a stout column, from which ribs extend into the corners and central points of the walls; the vault is thus well supported. Besides this, it has a tiny tribune, with a hermit's cell in it.

The wall paintings of San Baudel de Berlanga, now partly in the Prado (after being removed from the church and sent secretly to the United States), may be nearly the same age as the building itself, at least some of them. The most interesting are non-religious, with hunting scenes, a soldier with a lance and shield, an elephant, and so on. Painted in plain, smooth colors, they are noticeably Oriental in feeling, and help to show how Mozarabic art led on to Romanesque.

Thus Mozarabic emigration in the tenth century produced, in Christian territory, an art that in many ways recalls that of the Caliphate. And, similarly, the conquest of the Moorish areas of Spain from the eleventh century on produced another kind of art, thanks to the work of the Mudejars—that is, the Moslems who stayed on in the territory conquered by the Christians. Mudejarism was to penetrate deeply into Spanish art throughout the Middle Ages and even to persist until our own day. The

SYNAGOGUE OF EL TRÁNSITO, TOLEDO: DETAIL OF THE INTERIOR DECORATION. 1355-1357.

SYNAGOGUE OF CORDOVA: DETAIL OF THE INTERIOR DECORATION. 1314 OR 1315.

kind of work that at first was done only by Moorish artists was later learnt and assimilated by the Christians; and so the churches of different religions came to be linked in style, with fruitful results.

The best way to understand how these various religions coexisted is to take a closer look at the vigorous city of Toledo. Set in the center of the Peninsula, almost encircled by the gorges of the river Tagus, it stands on a rocky promontory and has steep, narrow streets. The privileged position of Toledo explains why it was already an important city under the Romans and the Visigoths. But its distinctive appearance was acquired between the Moslem invasion and the age of the Catholic kings. For, apart from everything else, it was here that the coexistence of Moslems, Christians and Jews had its happiest results. The churches of all three religions that still survive bear witness, above all, to the great unifying power of an art that was essentially Oriental.

Most of Toledo's early mosques have disappeared; but some are left which were converted into churches, and these help us to understand the spread of the art of the Caliphate. In the year 1000 a small mosque was built, on a square plan, today called El Cristo de la Luz. It embodies the characteristic features of Cordovan architecture:

semicircular, cusped, and horseshoe arches, and nine ribbed vaults, inspired by those of the Caliphate period; all on a very small scale, but beautifully executed in brick and stone. This mosque must have been the model for the mosque of Tornerías, which was probably built after the conquest of Toledo by Alfonso VI (1085). Some years ago, in the church of El Salvador, a series of arches was found that must have belonged to a Moorish mosque with five aisles.

Mudejar art flourished in Toledo side by side with Islamic work and in close connection with it. The Moslems who stayed on in the city when it was conquered impressed their own artistic style upon it, although many of their works were Christian churches; and there are a great many points of contact, here, between Mozarabic and Mudejar art. No building, perhaps, is as delightful as San Román. Its three aisles have horseshoe arches, with the voussoirs painted red and white, alternately, as in the Great Mosque of Cordova. Other things in the church, which are important both architecturally and decoratively, such as the tower, are stylistically more advanced. San Román was built in the thirteenth century within the Moorish tradition, and contrasts strongly with the Gothic cathedral built at the same time only a few yards away, in a typically European style. Brick, rubble masonry and plaster were nearly always used in the Mudejar buildings of Toledo, and Almohad elements appear in them as well, so that here the art of Seville is combined with that of Cordova. Toledan churches like Santiago del Arrabal, San Vicente, Santa Leocadia, and El Cristo de la Vega show how prevalent this style became.

In the synagogue of El Tránsito in Toledo, the rectangular plan is simple and functional, with a gallery on one side, reserved for the women. Mudejar influence is clearest in the decoration, in which there are elements both Arabic and Christian, as well as specifically Jewish: the braided ornamental plaster-work is typically Moorish; the escutcheons, with castles on them, record the fact that the synagogue was built and decorated for Samuel Levi, treasurer to King Peter the Cruel of Castile; specifically Jewish are the Hebrew inscriptions running along the edge of the frieze, which are arranged exactly as those of the Arabs were. Thus churches, mosques and synagogues, the places of worship of three religions, arose side by side in Toledo, combining stylistic features which give them an artistic unity over and above religious and political differences.

From the beginning of the twelfth century, the town of Sahagún (León) had a large colony of Mudejars (Moslems, that is, who remained in the areas reconquered by the Christians), and they left abundant evidence of their art in a number of churches, particularly in the kingdoms of León and Castile. The Mudejar church of San Lorenzo is one of the finest examples of "brick Romanesque," with its blind horseshoe arches decorating the apses. In the upper storeys of the square tower rising over the transept, however, there are elements that suggest the transition to Gothic.

APSE AND TOWER OF THE MUDEJAR CHURCH OF SAN LORENZO AT SAHAGÚN (LEÓN). 12TH-13TH CENTURY.

THE GREAT MOSQUE OF CORDOVA: RIBBED DOME OF THE MIHRAB (PRAYER RECESS). 965.

THE GREAT MOSQUE OF CORDOVA: RIBBED DOME OF THE CAPILLA REAL (ROYAL CHAPEL). 1258-1260.

Everywhere in Spain Mudejar art flourished vigorously, giving rise to an unmistakable style of its own. In order to understand how it spread, it is worth considering how certain elements permeated the Christian world.

The rib-vaults in the Great Mosque of Cordova, for instance, are echoed and imitated again and again in Spanish architecture. In the same mosque, beneath one of the domes of Al-Hakam II, is the Royal Chapel, built in the thirteenth century by Alfonso X, the Wise, for his own tomb. It is roofed by a rib-vault that keeps strictly to the style of the Caliphate, but there is more decoration on the walls and ceilings, which are covered completely by it. It has been suggested that this vault was in its turn influenced by one in the Almohad mosque of Seville. If this were quite certain, then here we would have an example of Cordovan structural features combined with decorative motifs that were basically Mozarabic, and were to be so much further developed at Granada in the Alhambra.

The vaults of the Caliphate period were taken over in Christian architecture. With ribs that do not cross in the center, they appear in the Talavera chapel in the old cathedral of Salamanca, in San Miguel de Almazán, Torres del Río and other Romanesque churches in Spain and even in France. There are also vaults of Moorish inspiration in the Mozarabic church of San Millán de la Cogolla and in the cathedral of Jaca, where the ribs at their center crossing clearly anticipate the Gothic ogives or diagonal ribs; thus demonstrating once again the important part Spain was to play in the Middle Ages as mediator between East and West.

Islamic influences appeared in many ways in styles as distinctly European as Romanesque. The eaves of the Great Mosque of Cordova, with their volute modillions,

ROMANESQUE MONASTERY OF SAN JUAN DE DUERO AT SORIA: VIEW OF THE CLOISTER. 12TH-13TH CENTURY.

78

The central dome over the crossing of the Romanesque cathedral of Zamora is flanked by four cylindrical turrets and covered with stone scales. It seems to suggest the presence here, in northwestern Spain, of an architect of Byzantine background who was active in the last third of the twelfth century and whose influence is felt in the neighboring towns of Toro and Salamanca. His work shows curious links with the French Romanesque architecture of Poitou.

CATHEDRAL OF ZAMORA: VIEW OF THE DOME OVER THE CROSSING. 1151-1174.

reappear—transmitted by way of Mozarabic art—in churches along the pilgrimage road to Santiago de Compostela, and even north of the Pyrenees. In the cloister of San Juan de Duero (Soria), there are three types of arches, horseshoe, semicircular and pointed, sometimes intersecting in the Moorish manner; there are also signs of Orientalism in the capitals and the decoration. In the transept of San Isidoro in León and in the Portada de Platerías in the cathedral of Santiago de Compostela there are cusped arches. Again at Compostela, the Portico de la Gloria, a magnificent work by Master Mateo, is full of details that suggest the Arab world.

On a more popular level, Moorish techniques and ornamental motifs were adapted in the case of smaller churches to structures that were specifically Romanesque. In many Castilian churches, built during the second half of the twelfth century and the early years of the thirteenth, we find what is called "brick Romanesque," which uses the Mudejar masons' favorite material and Islamic decorative rhythms; thus apses are decorated both inside and outside with blind arcades.

MUDEJAR CHURCH OF SANTA MARIA LA MAYOR AT LEBRIJA (SEVILLE): VIEW OF THE NORTH AISLE. 13TH CENTURY.

There was also a "Mudejar Gothic" in the churches built during the thirteenth, fourteenth and fifteenth centuries. In those of Andalusia, Orientalism is so strong that it is almost impossible to separate Gothic from specifically Moorish elements; such is the case in the beautiful parish church of Lebrija (province of Seville), where the horseshoe arch and vaults of various kinds show Almohad influence. In other Andalusian churches of a later date (some, like those in Granada, erected as late as the mid-sixteenth century), we find buildings whose structure is completely Gothic, with one or three aisles and pointed arches, but where the influence of Moorish woodwork is strong in ornate panelled ceilings; indeed, today it is probably the woodwork that recalls more clearly than anything the activities of the craftsman's workshops set up all over the Peninsula, and particularly in Andalusia.

Mudejar art is very varied, and this explains its originality in certain places and particular buildings. Around Andalusia the most remarkable example is the monastery of Guadalupe; its great cloisters have pointed horseshoe arches of Almohad type, and in the main cloister is a charming shrine that very happily combines Gothic and Moorish forms. Glazed ceramic motifs among the tracery give the shrine a vibrant note of color.

One of the most distinctive signs of Mudejar art in Aragon is the gleam of glazed tiles *(azulejos)*, which are used with great variety and beauty on towers, lanterns, apses and porches. The combination of brick and ceramic tiles gives character to the cathedral of Saragossa and the magnificent towers of El Salvador and San Martín at Teruel. Once again a fusion of Gothic and Mudejar expresses the artistic sensibility of a country that stands midway between East and West.

This survey of mosques, synagogues and churches might have ended in Moorish Granada, for there the final manifestation of Hispano-Arabic art was rich in ornamental forms and motifs that influenced the Christian world. But unfortunately the most important mosques of Granada have disappeared. Among the little that remains is the oratory of Partal, with its *mihrab* and its opulent decoration, which foreshadows the far greater richness of the Alhambra.

ART IN THE SERVICE OF LIFE

The history of the Middle Ages in Christian Spain was shaped in the main by religious influences, and an essentially spiritual feeling pervades most of the buildings that have come down to us, among which there are far more churches, monasteries and convents than buildings with a non-religious purpose. Indeed, hardly any secular architecture exists from before the year 1000, and the little that has reached us is, with a very few exceptions, military. Christians in the early Middle Ages seem to have divided their time between religion and warfare.

Spain's situation was paradoxical. Rome might symbolize the West, and Christianity in the Middle Ages might set itself up as the preserver of classical ideals; but in Spain it was the Moorish cities that showed what the ancient world had done to make life more agreeable. In Cordova, Seville and Granada, to mention only the most famous, there is still plenty to show how the Moors assimilated the lesson of Rome.

There is no doubt, all the same, that the Christians tried to maintain the ways of the ancient world, and even to organize their lives in accordance with them. The Germanic peoples who occupied the Peninsula lived very close to the classical culture; and we know that the Visigoths made definite efforts to take over Hispano-Roman forms of life. But, much more importantly, the kings of Asturias in the first Christian kingdom set up after the Moorish invasion of Spain laid great stress on secular architecture.

The kings who made Oviedo the capital of the first kingdom of the Reconquest seem to have felt an almost obsessive need to assert their power in fine buildings of both civil and religious architecture. The oldest accounts of the Asturian monarchy repeatedly mention the secular buildings of Alfonso II the Chaste, a contemporary of Charlemagne. Archaeological discoveries have confirmed that he built in Oviedo not merely churches, but a large, well-defended palace, fitted up with all the refinements of classical buildings; remains of its baths and drains have been found. Alfonso II wanted a court as brilliant as that of the Frankish emperor, and his buildings, designed for the everyday life of this world, answered the basic practical and political needs of a mountain kingdom, consolidating itself with its back to the Moorish world.

Alfonso II's palace in Oviedo can unfortunately be imagined only through a few archaeological remains. But happily the building which his successor, Ramiro I, erected halfway up the slopes of Monte Naranco, overlooking Oviedo, has come down to us almost intact. Its name—Santa María de Naranco—is misleading because, although for centuries it was used as one, it was not in fact built as a church. Alongside other

MUDEJAR TOWER OF EL SALVADOR AT TERUEL, WITH TILEWORK DECORATION. EARLY 13TH CENTURY.

buildings which have now disappeared, the king wanted a palace with a large reception hall occupying the whole of the main plan. With its wide, open galleries at the sides, the palace of Naranco is the most remarkable example in Europe of ninth-century civil architecture. Small though it is, no other surviving building of the time, in Spain or elsewhere, is as handsome. The rectangular hall, without its galleries, is over forty feet long by sixteen across; the galleries add about ten feet on either side.

The master of Naranco worked within the best architectural traditions, without losing sight of the lessons of Roman art. The hall is roofed with a barrel vault, reinforced with cross-ribs; it is the only ninth-century example of barrel vaulting left in the West, and it foreshadows, well in advance, what the Romanesque age was to bring, from the year 1000 onwards. The vaulting recalls that of such famous Roman buildings as the so-called Temple of Diana at Nîmes, but the similarity cannot be pressed, because the palace of Naranco is so original in design that many of its features have no antecedents. In the walls a blind arcade is supported by clusters of columns with cable patterns, harmoniously combining the structural with the ornamental. The wall spaces under the arches must have been frescoed. On the ground floor there are three separate rooms; it would seem that there was a bath in one of them, but the archaeological evidence is rather confused.

The palace of Naranco might be said to confirm the idea, already suggested, that Asturian art has an essentially classical background. Yet there are features in it that recall the East. The mouldings that decorate the arches and other architectural details have antecedents in Syrian buildings. The medallions that decorate the interior of the hall, with stylized plant and animal motifs, recall similar patterns in textiles and metalwork; and in particular there are links with the Sassanian art of Persia. The cable-patterned columns might suggest those of the Middle East, though earlier ones have been found in the Peninsula.

The forms used by the master of Naranco thus emphasize the coexistence of the classical spirit and the Oriental. In the middle of the ninth century, ideas that were to affect the art of the Peninsula and its secular architecture throughout the Middle Ages had already been well defined. But until the fifteenth century the finest pieces of architecture were produced in Moorish Spain. In the Christian kingdoms, during the Romanesque period and in the early days of Gothic, there are only a few exceptional buildings that matter, such as the Archbishop's Palace at Santiago de Compostela. And even this was not without traces of the East: the great hall, with its cross-vaults resting on richly carved brackets, has at the upper end ribs decorated with small horseshoe arches.

In the Moorish cities, the religious feeling that pervaded the whole of life did not prevent the development of civil architecture on a lavish scale. Cordova, the great

WEST FAÇADE OF SANTA MARIA DE NARANCO, NEAR OVIEDO. ASTURIAN ARCHITECTURE, 842-850.

ALMOHAD COURTYARD (PATIO DEL YESO) IN THE ALCAZAR OF SEVILLE: DETAIL OF THE ARCADES. 12TH CENTURY.

capital of the Arab world in the West, had many secular buildings which, judging from the accounts of Moorish chroniclers, must in magnificence have rivalled the mosque itself. We know that the caliphs built a great fortress or Alcazar, and not long ago the remains of their baths were discovered, in which the building technique of Roman baths was marvellously combined with their own delicate ornamentation.

In the tenth century Abderrahman III built an entire city a few miles from Cordova, in memory of one of his favorite concubines. Within its large precincts, Medina Azahra had a great many buildings at various levels, laid out around courtyards. Some of them had the Roman house plan; others were built on an Oriental plan, with large rooms for public receptions. The rich sculptural decorations (with geometrical motifs and stylized plant forms) give a good idea of the luxury of life there, and a reconstruction of the "Rich Hall" seems to justify the praises of contemporary chroniclers. They speak of artists who came from Baghdad, Damascus and Constantinople; of mosaics and marbles brought from the Byzantine world and from Rome; and of the gold, pearls, ivory, and rare woods in the palaces.

The Caliphate of Cordova came to an end with Al-Mansur's death in 1002, but the taste for ostentatious architecture persisted: buildings exaggeratedly large and opulent still arose. During the eleventh century Moorish Spain was broken up into more than a score of petty kingships (Taifas). Every important city became a tiny monarchy, and imposing citadels were built with sumptuous dwelling-houses within them. Few remains of these are left, unfortunately. Until the nineteenth century the main part of the Aljafería survived at Saragossa, a splendid fortified palace in which the stoutness of the outside walls must have contrasted with the richness of the interior; but in spite of the way it has recently been restored, the most interesting remains of this kind of building consist of capitals, arches and ornamental fragments scattered about in museums.

Something of the Alcazaba or citadel in Málaga has been saved, and from this we can imagine what the eleventh-century palace there must have been like. It included the pavilion called Cuartos de Granada which, though very much restored, suggests a light, open architecture, where the function of the cusped arches is decorative rather than structural; here again the patio is the center around which the rooms are laid out.

Remains of many other citadels survive, like the one at Almería, which unfortunately suffered a good deal of change when the city was occupied by the Christians and again quite recently when it was restored. All this makes it hard to picture the original Moorish building. Nothing remains of the Arab Alcazar at Toledo, possibly built on the site on which the later Alcazar arose in the sixteenth century. But civil architecture was still very much alive in Mudejar and Morisco buildings put up by the descendants of the Moors when Toledo was incorporated in the kingdom of Castile in 1086: for instance, the Taller del Moro, the Salón de Mesa, and the Palacios de Galiana.

The great Alcazar built in the twelfth century in Seville by the Almohad kings belongs to the same series of palaces. Very little remains of the original building: a vault in what was a flag room, and the façade of the Patio del Yeso. Both works are a link in the chain of architectural and decorative forms of Andalusian art, from its birth in Cordova till its death in Granada.

For Granada is the final stage in a long process, and at the same time the ripest fruit of the whole of medieval Islamic art enlisted in the service of life. In many ways Granada is a remarkable exception, for by some miracle the fragile architecture it produced has stood up well to the passage of time. The Alhambra is a tissue of contrasts: very stout walls with the lightest ornamental motifs imaginable; functional building

LOOKOUT OF DARAXA IN THE ALHAMBRA, GRANADA. 1353-1391.

treated in the most whimsical way, yet, incredibly, standing up to it. In the plan of what is called the Casa Real Vieja, the palace of the Moors, the arrangement of its masses seems at once unexpected and conventional; yet an inner logic appears to govern the series of patios and rooms that are arranged as independent units, but are finally moulded solidly together. The Alhambra is the most interesting medieval building in which the memory of Rome still persists (the courtyard is the axis around which the rooms of the house unfold), but embellished and steeped in the eastern feeling for life. It is conceived from within, in such a way that the solid outside walls give no idea of its magnificence. But it is also designed in a way that links it closely with the wonderful natural beauty of Granada; the views from its windows make it all seem part of the landscape, and the inner gardens carry all the beauty of nature right inside, into the very center of the building.

For centuries the Alhambra was used by Moslems and Christians, and this is the secret of its strange power of attraction. No other building reflects so well the triumph of the East in the West; no other shows as it does the intimate fusion of cultures in Spain during the Middle Ages.

The walled stronghold, with its stout square towers, is set on a hill that seems too frail to bear it. The most densely packed volumes are in the Alcazaba (citadel), built in the thirteenth century with a strongly military character. Behind it, side by side, are the two palaces, built in the fourteenth and fifteenth century, that enclose the Casa Real Vieja. They are the Palacio de Comares and the Palacio de los Leones, and their rooms are set round courtyards.

Every room and every piece of decoration in the Alhambra illustrates the principles of Islamic aesthetics. The interior space is broken up into a multitude of units: sometimes they form winding passages and sometimes square or rectangular halls. In each case the proportions vary: no strict rule governs the height of its ceilings or the size of its spaces, and contrast gives the most unexpected results. But in every case it is the visual effect that counts, and sometimes wonderful prospects are opened up, unrivalled in any other group of buildings. One can see right through a number of very disparate parts of the building at once, and look through patios and halls as far as the Albaicín quarter of the city, on another hill opposite the Alhambra.

The decoration of the Alhambra strikes a contrast with its sober architecture. Walls and roofs are completely covered with motifs in which the stylization of forms that began under the caliphs reaches its height. Geometrical and plant motifs are combined with inscriptions in the most varied compositions, heightened by colors and reliefs. The lower part of the walls is lined with a mosaic of enamelled tiles *(alicatados)*. Above these, the wall surface is encrusted with stucco reliefs whose ornamental patterns are so intricate that it is impossible for the eye to follow them. This decoration forms a kind of openwork strip above the arcades in the porticoes. The ceilings and the underside of arches are elaborately adorned with stucco pendants, making bold use of relief: through a clever use of concave and hanging elements, effects are achieved that suggest stalactites in caves.

Apart from the stucco reliefs, which of course are purely ornamental, there are other elements which are both decorative and functional: marble columns, for instance, and woodwork. The capitals take a form which marks the final stage in the evolution of the Roman type of Corinthian capital as used in Moorish art. The wooden doors and panelled ceilings use a "knot" technique, creating highly effective star-shaped patterns.

Water, which gives life to the entire Alhambra, must be added to all this. Fountains play, not only in the courtyards, but in the inner rooms. The Palace of Comares has a large pool in its center; the Palace of the Lions, a large fountain. Canals and ponds give character to the gardens. Water justified the baths, that legacy of the Romans in which a sense of the refinement of life seems to reach its height.

Turning to Christian Spain, we find a marked contrast. Men there were more concerned with eternal life than with everyday life, and so religious and secular architecture stood on very different levels. Until the fifteenth century we know of scarcely any palaces. In the castles what counts most is stout construction, not refinements that make life more comfortable.

This continued to be the case even into the later Middle Ages, when nobles built castles to assert their power to other nobles, and even to the king. Yet in the thirteenth century, when the Christians entered the valley of the Guadalquivir and conquered Cordova and Seville, they longed to copy the forms of life they found in the Andalusian cities. King Peter the Cruel, in the fourteenth century, set up his court in Seville and abandoned the Gothic style entirely when he enlarged the Moorish Alcazar: he closely followed the Almohad tradition and the art of the nearby kingdom of Granada. Profiting from his friendly relations with the Nasrid kings, he brought over a number of artists who had worked in the Alhambra and made the palace of Seville almost a replica of it.

This is why the Alcazar in Seville is rather more than a Mudejar building. It shows in particular the unity of spirit between people of different religions. In this same century the Jewish community (who were then on excellent terms with the monarch) built synagogues that followed the same aesthetic principles. In the palace of Peter the Cruel, the Hall of the Ambassadors, the Patio de las Doncellas, and the Cuarto de las Muñecas, in spite of later restorations, keep to the style of the Alhambra. The rooms are arranged around open spaces and communicate with the outside world through small winding passages, which were made so especially to safeguard the

HALL OF THE AMBASSADORS IN THE PALACE OF COMARES, IN THE ALHAMBRA, GRANADA. 1333-1391.

privacy of the interior. This explains why the main façade of the Alcazar in Seville is decorated with Almohad and Nasrid motifs, and is conceived in much the same way as the front of the Palace of Comares in the Alhambra. The outer gate opens on to a wall, and a winding passage leads from there to the courtyard.

No Spanish building of the late Middle Ages repays study as much as the Alcazar in Seville. But there is no doubt that the East had a profound effect on the mind of Christian kings and nobles. So, when castles were still being built in Castile, right into the fifteenth century, many of the principles of Moorish art survived. Even the stoutest Castilian strongholds have motifs of Mudejar origin in their surface decoration, and Mudejar influence sometimes even alters the concept of the fortress itself. Two of the most beautiful palace fortresses of the time, the castle of Coca and the Alcazar of Segovia, cannot be understood without bearing Moorish influence in mind.

CASTLE OF COCA (SEGOVIA): MUDEJAR WALL PAINTINGS IN THE TOWER OF PEDRO MATA. 15TH CENTURY.

VIEW OF THE CASTLE OF COCA (SEGOVIA). 15TH CENTURY.

The castle of Coca is girdled with several defensive walls and the entrances to these are planned in the Moorish way; a winding passage leads to the gate of each enclosure. The polygonal towers and turrets, the combinations of brick in several colors and even the wall paintings discovered a few years ago, give this castle an eastern air.

Many castles, marked by strong Mudejar influence, like that of Coca, show how military architecture progressed in the fifteenth century, adapting itself to a way of life that was growing steadily more polished. The nobles of Castile followed the example of their kings. The atmosphere in which the last medieval monarchs lived, from John II to the Catholic kings, was dominated by Moorish influences.

A brother of Isabella the Catholic, Henry IV, left proof of his love of eastern forms of life in a number of buildings in Segovia, and particularly in its spectacular Alcazar. A great fire that ravaged it in 1862, and an excessive amount of restoration, has to some extent obscured its quality; but here, in the heart of Castile, was a building worthy to rival the Alhambra itself. The landscape here, as in Granada, is decisively important. A river, the Eresma, and a turbulent stream poetically named El Clamores, have cut deep gorges and thrown into relief the great rocks on which the palace fortress rises. Segovia has been compared to a ship, whose rudder is the Roman aqueduct and whose prow, where the two rivers meet, is the medieval Alcazar. Its sober exterior does not prevent the walls and towers being set at various planes and levels, as happens in the Alhambra; and here too, the exterior contrasts with the decoration of its rooms. The Mudejar motifs, which have been discovered and restored, suggest a style of life influenced by Moorish ways: it appears that Henry IV even wore Oriental clothes. Carpets, curtains and furniture have, alas, disappeared, but they must have reflected the prevailing sense of life in this autumn of the Middle Ages.

The Catholic kings were not immune from these influences. Like her brother Henry IV, Queen Isabella, though so profoundly Christian, could not resist the spell of the Arab palaces. A few days after Ferdinand and Isabella entered Granada, at the end of January 1492, restoration work began in the Alhambra, and this did not mean a conflict with Islamic art, but a continuation of it. Even today it is hard to tell the difference between the work of the Moors and that of the Christians in the Alhambra. The artists who restored it in 1492 were direct descendants of those who, from the thirteenth to the fifteenth century, had been creating it. In the Court of the Lions the yoke and arrows, symbol of the Catholic kings, blend into the earlier decoration.

All these connections between the art of the medieval kingdoms, Moorish and Christian, confirm the triumph of the East in the West at the very time when the Renaissance was flourishing in Italy and beginning to make itself felt in the Peninsula. Though defeated on the battlefield, the Moors at least had the compensation of seeing their art carried on by their conquerors.

The Mudejar style was so attractive that it even filtered into the work of northern artists who came to Spain in the last third of the fifteenth century. These masters had been trained in the school of Flemish Gothic; but, dazzled perhaps by the profusion of ornament in Moorish art, they fell under its spell. One of the most representative examples of this architecture is the Infantado Palace at Guadalajara, built by Juan Guas in 1483 for Don Iñigo López de Mendoza, second Duke of Infantado. Few buildings better reflect the synthesis of East and West. The unity of Gothic and Moorish motifs is so perfect that they cannot be considered separately. An inscription on the doorway follows the outline of the pointed arches; it is thus given an ornamental value, like the inscriptions in the Alhambra. High on the façade are elements inspired by stucco pendants, and in the wonderful courtyard Gothic forms are overlaid with details of Moorish origin.

These are only a few examples of the wealth of buildings that give Spanish civil architecture on the eve of the Renaissance a character of its own. If the artists had not felt the influence of Mudejar traditions, the forms that came from Italy in the last decade of the fifteenth century might have been interpreted in a very different way. The preference for decoration, rather than construction, serves to confirm this.

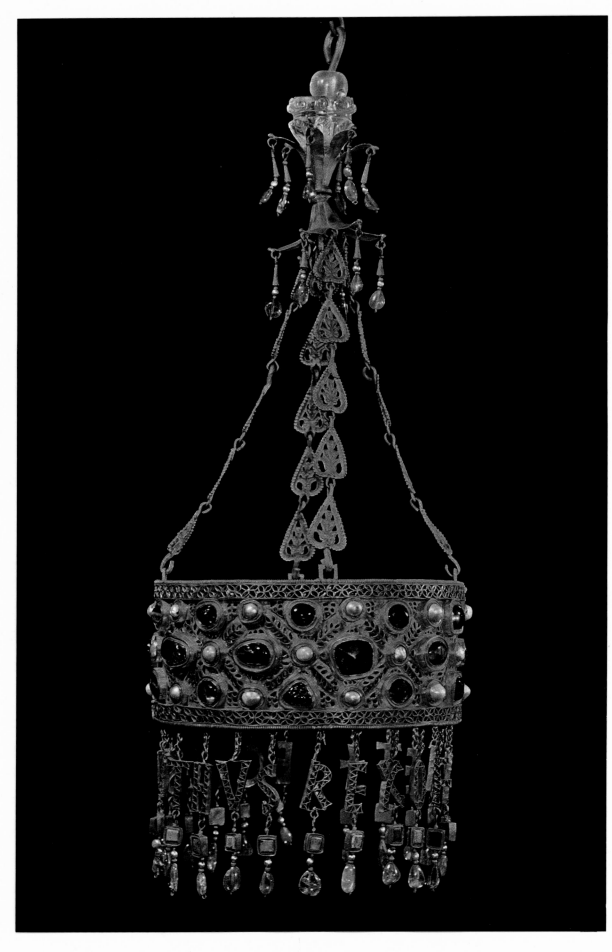

VISIGOTHIC CROWN OF RECCESVINTHUS FROM THE GUARRAZAR TREASURE (TOLEDO).
649-672. NATIONAL ARCHAEOLOGICAL MUSEUM, MADRID.

THE EMPHASIS ON DECORATION

If the terms East and West are compared in Spanish art, their most noticeable differences are to be seen in the field of decoration. In classical art, ornament was nearly always a secondary element. But in every style in which Oriental influences prevail, decoration penetrates the very essence of the work of art. For this reason no European country has as many works in which decoration is developed with such obsessive emphasis as Spain. Under the influence of the East, ornamental patterns cover every part of every surface; the same motif is repeated endlessly, and often all sense of measure or restraint is lost. The composition is governed by certain inner rhythms of a purely geometrical order, and the love of abstract design leads to the stylization even of plant and animal forms.

Throughout the centuries, and in centers that are artistically quite distinct, Spain produced works that were a result of eastern influences which had taken firm root. Not all of these, though, came from the Mohammedan world. The previous contacts of the Germanic invaders (above all the Goths) with countries east of Italy, the direct penetration into the Christian kingdoms of medieval Spain of elements from Syria and Byzantium, meant further links with the East.

The final result of these contacts (which, as we saw, had many precedents in ancient times) resulted in a Spanish tendency, in every age, to emphasize ornament. It is through the decorative arts and certain adjuncts of architecture that ornamental forms are diffused. Jewelry, ivories, bronzes, ceramics, textiles and miniatures, panelling and frescoes, all testify unmistakably to the presence of the East in the West.

Visigothic art offers the first of countless examples. Before the Moslems came, Visigothic jewelry shows a kind of synthesis of the various ornamental techniques used in the ancient world. The treasures of Guarrazar (Toledo) and Torredonjimeno (Jaén), discovered in 1859 and 1926 respectively, contain a splendid collection, which has suffered many vicissitudes: part of it was stolen from the Royal Armory in Madrid; part of it, after a time in the Cluny Museum in Paris, was exchanged for something else and returned to Spain (National Archaeological Museum, Madrid). The most important part of both these treasures consisted of a number of votive crowns (hung up as offerings in churches) and jewelled crosses. Each one of these shows individual forms and techniques. Some are made of soldered pieces, in latticework, with stones set at the intersections; others are made of flat strips of gold on which the stones are directly encrusted; in others the decoration is achieved by perforating or embossing the metal, and in some cases beautiful color effects are achieved by enamel inlays (according to the so-called cloisonné technique) forming small geometrical patterns.

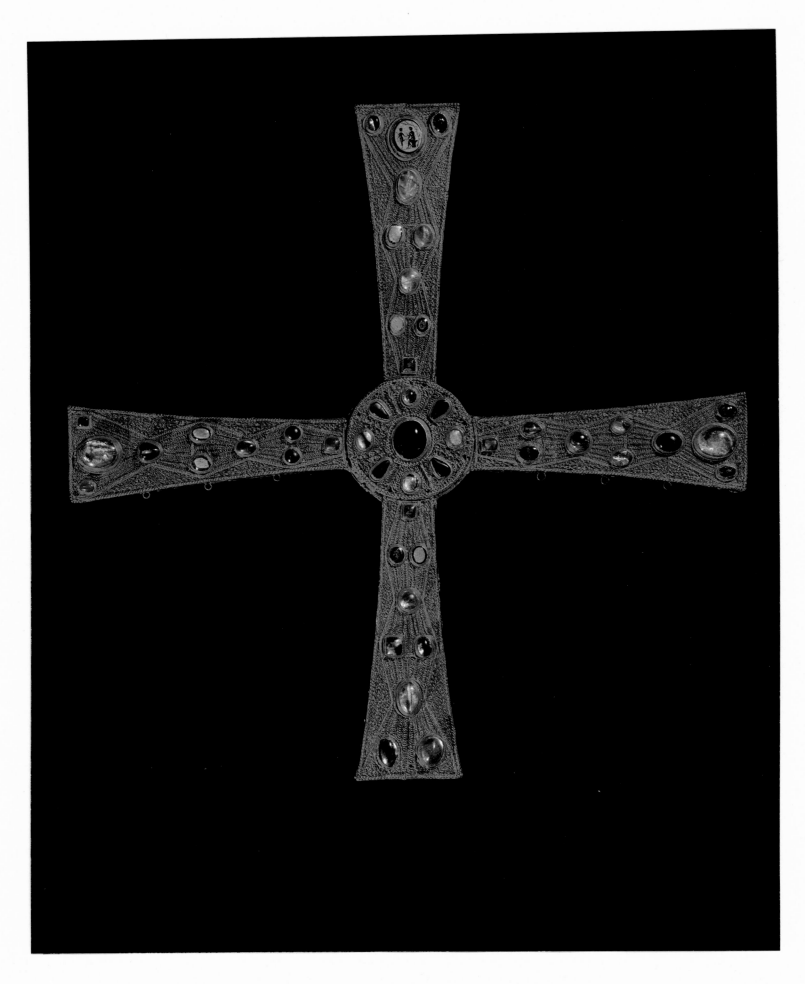

CROSS OF THE ANGELS. 808. CÁMARA SANTA, OVIEDO CATHEDRAL.

The Cross of the Angels (808), which has arms of equal length, trapezoidal in shape, is decorated with very fine gold filigree work. Rows of precious stones set in the arms and central disk add to the sense of richness, and there are several cameos with pagan subjects, which give a touch of classicism to a work that is strongly stamped with Byzantine feeling. On the back is a votive inscription. The Cross of Victory, made a hundred years later, differs in technique and in form. The vertical arm is longer and the ends are decorated with cusps. Its enamels and precious stones are astonishingly rich; very delicate figures of animals are finely delineated on the enamels.

The crucifix which Ferdinand I, king of Castile and León, and his wife Sancha gave to the collegiate church in León, in the year 1063, is no doubt the masterpiece of Leonese ivory carving. It has recently been discovered that the torso of Christ was used as a reliquary. Iconographically, the figure is of Byzantine origin, but it was taken over by Romanesque artists. Jesus is represented alive, with wide-open eyes (inset with sapphires), without any expression of suffering. The arms of the cross are delicately carved with a profusion of men and animals interlaced, symbolizing the fight against evil and the resurrection of the dead. Beneath the feet is the stooping figure of Adam, and at the very bottom are the names of the royal donors: FREDINANDUS REX and SANCIA REGINA. On the back are the symbols of the Evangelists, the Lamb of God, and a motley crowd of figures, real and imaginary, surrounded by stems curving into circles. Andalusian influence is confirmed by a significant fact: remains of gold leaf have been detected on the ivory ground around some of the figures, and gold leaf was also found a few years ago in the decorations discovered in the baths of the caliph at Cordova.

The crowns from Guarrazar and Torredonjimeno also have chains with which to hang them from the ceiling, and pendants that decorate the lower part of them. They are usually hung up by these chains; but in some cases remains of clasps can be seen, once used to fasten them at the breast.

The masterpiece of Visigothic jewelry is the Guarrazar crown, which has the words RECCESVINTHVS REX OFFERET on the lower part of it in dangling letters, and can be dated between the years 649 and 672. It is made of two semicircular pieces, joined, each with a double veneer of gold to make it the more solid. On the edges are emeralds set in rings, and on the wide central strip stalks with leaves set crosswise are suggested by the simple process of leaving gaps where the leaves ought to be. Three rows of pearls and sapphires are set in the gold sheets with soldered rings. The chains, set in at four points, and afterwards joined in a kind of double flower, have heartshaped links. The dangling letters have triangular containers for the enamels; and still more stones, enclosed in polished gems and pearls, are set in these letters.

Even without going into more detail, the quality and originality of this jewelled crown are quite obvious; and so is its stylistic connection with Byzantine works, especially in the way the stones and gold are combined. The cross that hangs from the crown is encrusted with stones and pearls (these are on the ends of the arms), and has dangling additions much like those that hang from the letters. What is most surprising of all is the way in which the stones are held by small claws. On the back are remains of a clasp that meant it could be used as a pectoral cross. Although it is considered slightly earlier than the crown, and even more closely linked with Byzantine works, it fits perfectly with seventh-century Visigothic jewelry.

In other Visigothic objects made in metal we find connections with eastern works, such as those from south Russia and the Balkans. There are, for instance, brooches in the shape of eagles: the eagles are very stylized, with the body facing forwards and the head in profile; they are generally covered with enamel inlays. This type of work has connections with other Ostrogothic works, such as those in the treasure of Petrosa (Rumania), which is so hard to place, stylistically. Of course, as jewelry is so small and easily carried, it may influence techniques and types of decoration in places very far removed from one another.

The kingdom of Asturias, which was to some extent nourished by Visigothic and Hispano-Roman traditions, produced some outstanding jewelry. Some of it suggests artistic links with other peoples. Although not a great deal of it has survived, the techniques and forms are so varied, and the time covered is so great, that the whole collection is extremely valuable. Most beautifully made of all is the Cross of the Angels preserved in the Cámara Santa of Oviedo cathedral. Through an inscription on the back, we know that it was given by King Alfonso II the Chaste in 808.

THE ALHAMBRA BASIN. LATE 10TH CENTURY. MARBLE. ALHAMBRA MUSEUM, GRANADA.

The eagles and animals that decorate the Alhambra basin can be found as far back as the third millennium B.C. in Sumerian art; on the plaque of Dudu, for instance, in the Louvre. The theme may have come to the Moslem world through figured textiles, metalwork, ivory carving or painted pottery. Shown above is one of the narrow sides of the basin, which is decorated with reliefs on all four sides. The smooth central part must have been fitted with some metal ornament joined to the water-spout, which may have been similar in form to the bronze deer in the Cordova museum illustrated on page 107. Apart from this basin, two others are known which have reliefs with very similar eagle-shaped forms: one, from Medina Azahra, is in the National Archaeological Museum, Madrid; the other was found in the Medrese (seminary) of Marrakesh in Morocco. By comparison with these, the Alhambra basin can be dated to the last years of the tenth century; on one side of it is an inscription dated 1306, but this probably went to replace the original inscription.

The casket of the Agates is a masterpiece of the goldsmith's art. It consists of three distinct parts. The bottom is made of a plate of embossed silver, with a cross and the symbols of the Evangelists in the center; a lengthy inscription runs around the edge. The casket rested on four spherical knobs. The eagle of St John, the angel of St Matthew, the lion of St Mark and the bull of St Luke emerge from circles with curved radii, a motif which has a great many antecedents in Spain, for instance in pre-Roman gold and silver work and in some reliefs in the Visigothic church of San Juan de Baños (Palencia). The sides of the casket are plated with very thin sheets of gold; set in these are onyxes surrounded by relief patterns. As for the lid, a gold plate richly decorated with enamels and precious stones, it is evidently taken from some other, earlier work. Professor Schlunk has related it to the cover of the Lindau Gospel Book (Morgan Library, New York) and dated it to the middle of the ninth century. The enamels represent stylized figures of birds—a motif of eastern origin. Red garnets set in narrow bands and other larger stones enhance the beauty of the enamelled plaque in the center, which measures six by four inches. The total length of the casket is about nineteen inches; it stands just under eight inches high.

CASKET OF THE AGATES, BOTTOM: EMBOSSED SILVER PLATE. 910. CÁMARA SANTA, OVIEDO CATHEDRAL.

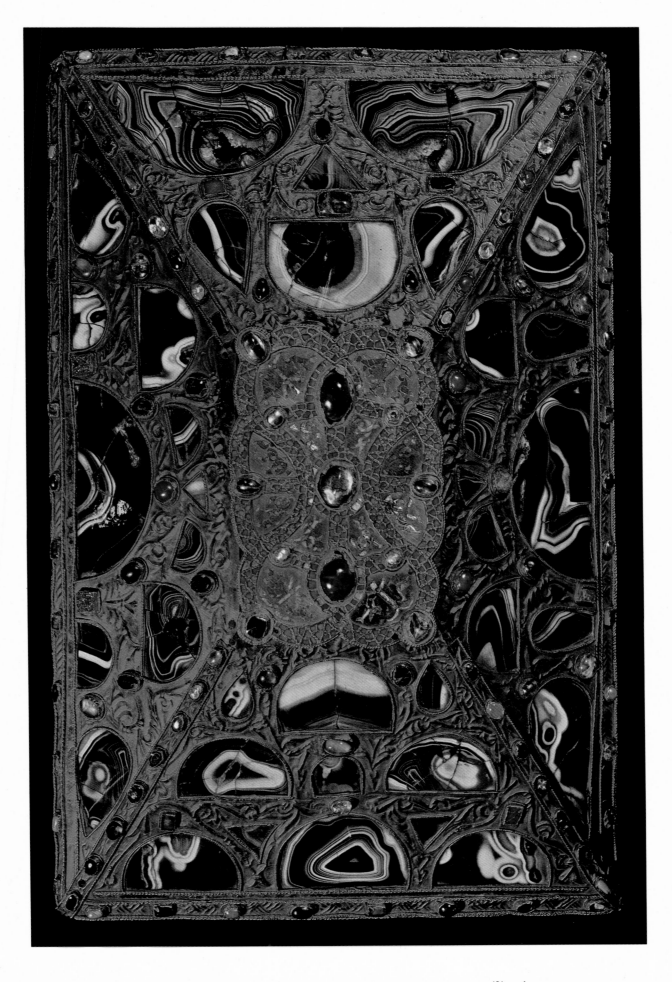

CASKET OF THE AGATES, LID: ENAMELLED GOLD PLATE INLAID WITH STONES. 9TH CENTURY (?). CÁMARA SANTA, OVIEDO CATHEDRAL.

Exactly a century after it comes the Cross of Victory, made to the order of King Alfonso III the Great in a workshop located in the castle of Gauzón; this is recorded in an inscription on the back of it. The third masterpiece of Asturian jewelry is a small chest inlaid with agates, given to Oviedo cathedral in the year 910 (two years after the Cross of Victory) by Prince Fruela.

The faint Moorish influences found in Asturian works recall the art of the Caliphate. But Moorish jewelry seems to have had a brief flowering. The Andalusians, like the Arab peoples, were attracted by jewels, but very few of theirs have reached us. A few small finds in the provinces of Cordova, Granada and Almería show the existence of an outstanding art that had completely mastered the techniques of filigree and embossed work. Perhaps the most beautiful specimens of Moorish metalwork are the bronzes.

The finest piece, found in Medina Azahra, is now in the Cordova Museum: a deer made to decorate a fountain. The figure is hollow, and the water must have flowed out of its mouth. It is soberly modelled, with short legs, a cylindrical trunk and a thick neck; this gives it a static appearance that suited its function. Slender stalks, enfolding leaves, make a typically Moorish ornamental motif that is repeated nearly all over its body. Only sixteen inches high, it shows what the fountains in the Cordovan palaces must have been like, with marble basins surmounted by animals like this one, which the chroniclers described and praised. Originally the Cordovan deer must have been gilt; this can be deduced not just from a careful examination of it but from a comparison with another less valuable statue in the National Archaeological Museum in Madrid.

The most brilliant phase of Moorish decoration in small objects is found in ivory carvings. We know that in the tenth century workshops producing ivories of very fine quality were active in Cordova and Cuenca. The important collection of small chests and ivory jars that has been preserved proves how untrue the idea is that Arabic art is systematically opposed to representing the human form. The scenes carved on them are clearly anecdotal, with hunters, musicians, warriors and so on; these are enclosed in compositions that consist of animals or geometrical patterns and stylized plants. The surfaces are always completely covered with decoration, and the inscriptions, which have a decorative value themselves, often help to document them.

The Cuenca workshops produced objects like the ivory caskets from Silos and Palencia (today in the museums of Burgos and Madrid) which are remarkable for the unusual depth of their relief. The repertory of themes, on the other hand, is much the same as on the Cordova ivories: stylized stems and leaves, confronted animals, hunting scenes, inscriptions with a decorative purpose, and so on. But there are many hybrid animals as well, such as winged or bird-headed quadrupeds. In every case they recall figures that are found far back in the ancient world, in the art of the Middle East.

BRONZE DEER FROM MEDINA AZAHRA, NEAR CORDOVA. IOTH CENTURY. ARCHAEOLOGICAL MUSEUM, CORDOVA.

IVORY JAR FROM ZAMORA. 964. NATIONAL ARCHAEOLOGICAL MUSEUM, MADRID.

The ivory jar from Zamora was made in the year 964 for a favorite concubine of the caliph Al-Hakam II. It has a cylindrical body and a conical lid with an Arabic inscription on it. Its decoration, as Gómez-Moreno has pointed out, is similar to that on the great Moorish buildings of the Caliphate period. Stalks that develop rhythmically and end in stylized leaves or floral motifs predominate, and in the spaces between them are deer, peacocks and other birds. The composition is remarkable for its careful symmetry. Many of its ornamental elements are Byzantine in origin. Here we are still a long way from the abstract patterns that were to prevail in the final periods of Moorish art.

The Leire casket is one of the most beautiful pieces of Cordovan ivory carving. Since its recent cleaning, Jorge Navascués has made a careful study of it and greatly enlarged our knowledge of this work. It represents the last caliph of Cordova, Hisham II, although one of the horses bears the mark of Al-Mansur's stables. The casket was made as a present for one of Al-Mansur's sons in 1005, being offered to him by a eunuch in his service who later became king of Almería. We know too that it was carved by an artist named Faray, with the help of his pupils. In addition to the same motifs that appear on the Zamora jar, it is decorated with a series of scenes enclosed in cusped circles, showing musicians, figures with fruit or flasks, horsemen or elephants fighting, hunters, etc. The origins of these scenes can be found in the figured textiles of Sassanian Persia.

The Tortosa casket is decorated with ivory inlays. On the front and on the lid are a series of animals surrounded by foliage patterns, each animal being enclosed in a large circular medallion. The beauty of the outlined motifs makes up for the lack of relief. The plant motifs are carved with particular delicacy.

IVORY PLAQUES FROM THE CASKET OF THE BEATITUDES. FIRST HALF OF THE IITH CENTURY.
NATIONAL ARCHAEOLOGICAL MUSEUM, MADRID.

After the fall of the Caliphate of Cordova, Moorish ivory carving maintained its traditions for some time, throughout the eleventh century. Its aftermath can be seen mainly in Christian Spain. There, in the late twelfth or early thirteenth century, the technique of marquetry, using inlays of ivory, was developed, and some very delicate work resulted, following methods similar to those of mosaic or inlaid tiling. The two most important examples are in the National Archaeological Museum, Madrid (the small chest from San Isidoro in León) and the cathedral of Tortosa (Tarragona).

The ivory-work of Cordova and Cuenca must have made its impact on Christian art by way of the Mozarabs, as a result of the large-scale emigration in the tenth and eleventh centuries to the areas reconquered from the Moors. The ivories produced in the workshops of León and Castile show how Moorish art brought its influence to bear on Romanesque. The crucifix of King Ferdinand I of Castile is the finest of the eleventh-century Spanish ivories, but the León workshops turned out other very interesting works, like the San Isidoro casket, dated 1059 (which has figures framed by horseshoe arches, a sure sign of Mozarabic influence), and the so-called casket of the Beatitudes in the National Archaeological Museum.

Another important workshop was at San Millán de la Cogolla (Logroño), where an extremely interesting Mozarabic church is still preserved. The San Millán ivories concentrate less on ornament than on narrative scenes. This is so, for instance, in the small chest dedicated to the titular saint. Its panels show several buildings with horseshoe arches. Thus Moorish styles and techniques continued to be taken over in Christian art.

Spanish metalwork in the eleventh century also shows links between East and West, and testifies to the vitality of Spanish Romanesque, thanks to the stimulus of Andalusian influences. Specifically Christian themes are coupled with decorative elements of Islamic origin. An example is the very fine reliquary shrine in Oviedo cathedral. It can be dated around 1075. Its gilded silver front and lid combine the two techniques of niello and embossed work. Mozarabic features are unmistakable here, and among details of Andalusian origin there is a Cufic inscription serving as a hall-mark on the front. The small silver shrine of Bishop Arianus, also in Oviedo cathedral, has a similar inscription on the upper part which, up to a point, balances the letters of the bishop's name inscribed on the lower part. Mozarabic details can be detected in many other works as varied as the Celanova altar and the processional cross of Mansilla de la Sierra.

Two other outstanding works are the Silos chalice, of the mid-eleventh century, and the cover of the Gospel Book of Queen Felicia (1063-1086); the latter is in the Metropolitan Museum, New York. A detail links these two works: the decoration in filigree with stones superimposed on it, that recalls the technique used in the Cross of the Angels. The chalice preserved in the monastery of Santo Domingo de Silos is remarkable for its size and for the fact that its base and cup are decorated with a series of horseshoe arches, which have been thought to suggest the church of the Holy Sepulchre in Jerusalem.

The diffusion, through the Mozarabs, of Moorish decoration in the Christian kingdoms is not confined to ivory carving and metalwork. It also extends to miniature painting —notably the miniatures in the so-called Beatus manuscripts. These are a large group of illuminated manuscripts containing the commentaries on the Book of Revelation and the Book of Daniel written in the eighth century by a monk named Beatus at the

MOZARABIC MINIATURE BY MARTINUS ILLUSTRATING THE APOCALYPSE COMMENTARIES OF BEATUS OF LIÉBANA. 1086.
FOLIO 108 RECTO, CODEX NO. I, CATHEDRAL LIBRARY, EL BURGO DE OSMA (SORIA).

MOZARABIC MINIATURE BY MARTINUS ILLUSTRATING THE APOCALYPSE COMMENTARIES OF BEATUS OF LIÉBANA. 1086.
FOLIO 145 VERSO, CODEX NO. I, CATHEDRAL LIBRARY, EL BURGO DE OSMA (SORIA).

monastery of Liébana in the old kingdom of León. His commentaries became so popular that from the ninth to the twelfth century they were copied from one monastery to another. The scribes did not merely reproduce the text: they collaborated with gifted and imaginative illustrators who were thoroughly familiar with the decorative styles of Carolingian and Moorish art. The miniatures show Orientalism in many ways—the stylization of plant forms, certain interlace patterns, the frames with horseshoe arches, some aspects of the composition, and the color contrasts. Here again Spain offers a remarkable synthesis between East and West, and Moorish forms are enlisted in the service of Christian art.

The Beatus manuscripts have provoked some heated controversy in the past few years. Camón Aznar has emphasized the western character of the text; the commentaries on the Apocalypse were indeed written, like Beatus' other works, to combat the adoptionist heresy, which was widespread among the Mozarabs. But once again Spanish art gave rise to a paradox: the illustrations, in spite of their undoubted connection with works from north of the Pyrenees, are steeped in Islamic elements. The stylistic evolution of the Beatus miniatures in the course of three centuries reflects the artists' sensitive reaction to the trends of their time. A few examples illustrate the transition from Mozarabic to Romanesque.

The first important Beatus manuscript was illustrated by a powerful artist named Magius, probably in the second quarter of the tenth century; written, it would seem, at the monastery of San Miguel de Escalada (León), it is now in the Morgan Library, New York. The artist reveals a certain Byzantine strain, a keen sense of movement, and particular sensibility in suggesting landscape; the Mozarabic element appears above all in his linear arabesques and his habit of framing his figures in horseshoe arches. The path thus marked out is continued by the Távara Beatus, begun perhaps by Magius but completed by his pupil Emetrius between 968 and 970.

The Távara Beatus is preserved in the National Archives in Madrid. Quite apart from its stylistic interest, it has a special documentary value because one of its miniatures represents the monastery tower in some detail, with its horseshoe arches, the ladders connecting one storey with another (there are no stairs), its two bells, and its checkered mural decoration of different colored tiles. Built against the tower is the scriptorium in which two illuminators can be seen at work. The ingenuous device of representing the figures as if the walls were transparent indicates the importance Emetrius attached to the anecdotal element. The school of Magius was continued in the Valcavado Beatus, in the university of Valladolid, and another at La Seo de Urgel. The former was illuminated in 970 by an artist named Oveco. One of his miniatures, representing the Adoration of the Lamb, shows the symbols of the Evangelists looking out above circular forms, as on the small chest inlaid with agates in Oviedo cathedral. This motif, here imbued with Orientalism, has Visigothic antecedents too, and confirms the rich variety of influences exerted on Spanish art in the early Middle Ages. Five years later than the Távara and Valcavado manuscripts is the Beatus in Gerona cathedral, which may have been illuminated in Castile, though its miniatures show a school distinct from that of Magius. This manuscript, which had no influence on the Catalan Bibles, is recalled in the Turin Beatus of the early twelfth century.

Other Mozarabic manuscripts, outside the Beatus group, offer many examples of Oriental forms, combined in some cases with obvious Nordic strains. But no more need be said here of these tenth-century miniatures. Of more interest is the late eleventh-century Beatus manuscript of El Burgo de Osma, which marks the appearance of Romanesque features. Signed by an artist named Martinus and dated 1086, it is probably the masterpiece of Spanish art in this century. Its large miniatures show a powerful vein of expressionist feeling and have a plastic vigor of wholly western origin; yet Mozarabic traditions persist in the arabesques of the calligraphy and in images of an Oriental type.

The emphasis on decoration also appears in other Moorish works that penetrated the Christian world. Figured textiles came from Andalusia to Castile throughout the Middle Ages, and Arab Spain became a link between Europe and the Middle Eastern countries that traded with the Far East. This may explain the importance of the silk industry and the spread of fabrics with designs of eastern origin. Egyptian and Persian weavers had particular influence in Andalusia and from the time of the Caliphate to the Granada period the weaving industry was vigorously maintained by the Moslems; their products, exported to the Christian kingdoms, seem to have been very highly esteemed. This was shown in 1944 when the tombs of Alfonso VIII and his descendants were discovered in the convent of Las Huelgas at Burgos: Arab textiles abounded in the coffins and clothes of the royal family. As a result of these discoveries a museum that is unique of its kind was opened at Las Huelgas.

The number of fabrics preserved is unfortunately very small and in most cases fragments are all that remain. The earliest remnant of the costumes worn by the Moorish rulers (which must have been very opulent) dates from the end of the tenth century. It is a strip of linen, 43 inches long and 16 inches wide, dedicated to the caliph Hisham II, whose prime minister was Al-Mansur. Very likely it was part of a turban of fine linen edged with silk. The inscription runs along both sides, and in hexagonal medallions on the central band there are various motifs, chiefly animals (quadrupeds and birds); but there are also two human figures, one of them holding a flask, the other shown in half length.

A later work is the so-called banner of Las Navas de Tolosa, preserved in the convent of Las Huelgas at Burgos. It is not known for certain what its original use was. Some have thought it to be a fragment of the tent of the Moorish leader defeated by

Alfonso VIII in 1212 in one of the most decisive battles of the Reconquest, the battle of Las Navas de Tolosa. But it was probably a flag of the Almohad army which was routed there. In any case, it is a splendid piece of cloth, over ten feet by six and richly decorated, with the ornamentation incorporated in the woof, by the use of the tapestry technique. Gold and silk threads of many colors are woven into the fabric, which has a circle in the middle, surrounded by spandrels and bands that form a square, and enclosing the decorative motifs within it. Bands have been added along the top and bottom, and the lower edge is bordered by eight pointed scallops. As is usual in Mohammedan art, geometric elements and stylized plant forms are combined with inscriptions that, according to Arabic tradition, repeat certain prayers.

The Orientalism of Spanish medieval textiles can be seen even in works that are clearly Christian and whose value is basically anecdotal, such as the tapestry of the Creation in Gerona cathedral. It is really an embroidered cloth, and is of basic importance in Romanesque art, as regards both its imagery and style. Unfortunately parts of it, on the right and at the bottom, have been lost and we can only guess what they may have been like. The circle inscribed in a square appears in the composition; the central part is occupied by the Pantocrator, around whom the Creation scenes, presided over by the Holy Ghost, are set in eight sections. In the spandrels between the circle

TURBAN OF HISHAM II: LINEN EDGED WITH SILK. 10TH CENTURY. ROYAL ACADEMY OF HISTORY, MADRID.

BANNER OF LAS NAVAS DE TOLOSA. 12TH-13TH CENTURY. CONVENT OF LAS HUELGAS, BURGOS.

and the edges are symbols of the winds; in the lower part, scenes showing the finding of the Cross partially remain; and finally, along the borders, are a series of pictures, most of which describe the months of the year.

The origin of this composition must be sought in classical works, in particular mosaic pavements like the one from Carthage, now in the British Museum. But there is no doubt that these forms were used again in the Byzantine world, where domes, either painted or decorated with mosaic, suggested the idea of the circle. Miniatures and textiles earlier than this tapestry had already shown the association of circles and squares, but the whole composition in the cathedral of Gerona is unusual. Pedro de Palol considers it a typically Catalan work from the end of the eleventh or the first half of the twelfth century. Very likely it is; and its special interest is that it unites a number of western and eastern trends. Motifs of Byzantine or Islamic origin are combined with others in the classical tradition, or still others from north of the Pyrenees. The Genesis mosaic in St Mark's in Venice (thirteenth century) has remarkable similarities with the Gerona tapestry. It may well be that the two works derive from a common source.

But it was in Moorish Spain, in many art forms, that eastern decoration found full scope to express itself. Bronzes and ivories were very important in tenth-century Cordova, but in the time of the Caliphate the art of ceramics, which was to reach its height in the next few centuries, was just beginning. Glazing, which may have been invented in ancient Egypt, was the most important ceramic technique brought in from the Islamic world, and Andalusia soon adopted it. In the tenth century there were two main pottery-making centers, at Elvira (Granada) and Azahra (Cordova), which both showed Oriental influences.

Glazed wares reached their height between the thirteenth and fifteenth centuries, and it was in Málaga that the best work of Moorish Spain was done. It is obvious that from at least 1240 the potters of Málaga used gold enamel, and it seems that from very early times their products were exported to places as far afield as Italy and Egypt. Travellers and chroniclers praised them highly until as late as the sixteenth century, and indeed the name Málaga comes from the Italian word *maiolica*, which means, in fact, glazed ceramics.

Like the other arts, ceramic wares showed a curious cross between the Mohammedan and the Christian worlds. In Valencia, which traded actively with the Mediterranean countries, the potteries of Paterna and Manises, which were very famous by the second half of the fourteenth century, were started soon after the conquest of the city by James I of Aragon in 1232. In this way, the Mohammedan style was passed on unmodified to what might be called Mudejar works, and even individual pieces are all too easy to confuse.

TAPESTRY OF THE CREATION: EMBROIDERED CLOTH. IITH-12TH CENTURY. CHAPTER OF GERONA CATHEDRAL.

Glazed ceramics very soon came to play an important part in the decoration of buildings. The most delicate work was produced by an elaborate mosaic of lustred tiles of different shapes and sizes, called *alicatados*; the walls of the Alhambra, as we have seen, are decorated with them.

In Granada the oldest and finest tiling of this kind is certainly that in the Cuarto Real de Santo Domingo; and there are some beautiful examples of tilework mosaics in the Alcazar of Seville and other late medieval buildings where Moorish influence made itself felt. The patterns made by combining tiles of various sizes and colors are admirable. They have antecedents in Roman and Byzantine mosaics, and their abstract designs seem to anticipate the non-representational art of our time.

Owing to the difficulty of fitting together such intricate patterns, these tiles were gradually superseded in the later Middle Ages by *azulejos*—square or rectangular tiles which were much easier to handle. The use of *azulejos*, ornamented with Moorish motifs, spread all over Spain and has continued to the present day.

The Moorish potters of Málaga produced a large quantity of vessels with characteristic forms: high-necked jars, large bowls, and in particular some magnificent tall vases that were purely decorative. Perhaps the most beautiful is the one known as the Alhambra Vase; others are scattered in museums and collections in Spain, Italy, Switzerland, Germany, Sweden, Russia and the United States. But the Alhambra Vase in Granada is particularly fine. It stands over four feet high, and although it has been damaged (it has lost a handle and some of its ornamentation) its elegant designs and blue and gold coloring are still enchanting. With its extreme calligraphic precision, the decoration seems to have been inspired by a Persian miniature. On the shoulder, between the handles, stylized gazelles are depicted face to face.

The very fine Manises wares of Valencia show a further development of Moorish influences. The large plates with metallic lustres are richly adorned with arabesques, heraldic emblems, human figures, inscriptions (the Ave Maria, for example) and narrative scenes. The plate reproduced here shows on both sides men in boats and fish cleaving the waves. Two men are shooting arrows at birds—waterfowl, perhaps, in the lagoons of Valencia. The plant forms appear to be the characteristic flora of the lagoons. The plate has a diameter of 18½ inches and dates to the fifteenth century.

Moorish art forms and ornamental techniques are not limited to metalwork, ivories, textiles and ceramics. Fine decorative work was also done in other media—marble plaques for instance, and even such common materials as limestone and plaster; there are magnificent examples of such mural decorations in the mosque of Cordova and at Medina Azahra. Under the Caliphate an art form began that soon grew and spread: it transposed to large surfaces what had already been done on a small scale in ivory carvings. At Cordova this decorative art was at first naturalistic; later this naturalism disappears. The delicately wrought fragments found there a few years ago in the baths of the caliphs are richly colored and plated with gold leaf.

At Medina Azahra countless pieces of carved marble and limestone suggest how dazzling must have been this palace-city before its destruction in the eleventh century. The elaborate column bases and capitals prove once again that Cordova was the starting point of that decorative art which culminated so brilliantly at Granada.

THE ALHAMBRA VASE. LUSTRED WARE. SECOND HALF OF THE 15TH CENTURY. ALHAMBRA MUSEUM, GRANADA.

FAIENCE PLATE FROM MANISES (VALENCIA). 15TH CENTURY. INSTITUTO DE VALENCIA DE DON JUAN, MADRID.

At Granada, first in the villa known as the Cuarto Real de Santo Domingo, then in the Alhambra, the colorful stucco reliefs and stalactite ornaments demonstrate the decorative possibilities of plaster when it is skillfully and imaginatively used. The Generalife, or summer palace of the Moorish kings, shows how the mural decorations were renewed when necessary. For all their fragility, they have stood up well to the passage of time.

Instead of tilework mosaics and stucco reliefs, walls were sometimes decorated with paintings, but unfortunately very few have survived from Arab times. Some interesting Mudejar murals remain, though, such as the dadoes in Santo Domingo Real in Segovia and the Archaeological Museum in Cordova, painted in imitation of arabesque tilework *(alicatados)* but also containing figures. The restoration of the castle of Coca, completed in 1958, brought to light a wealth of ornamental paintings in the passages and inner rooms. Geometrical compositions predominate, often emphasizing architectural elements, such as arches with painted voussoirs. Their style on the whole is unsophisticated, but here and there, as in a room in the tower of Pedro Mata, the hand of a more sensitive and skillful artist can be distinguished. Above a dado decorated with an interlace pattern, he depicted a series of intersecting stilted arches; under them are tall stalks with leaves and some simple jugs that have given the room its name. It is curious to observe how the artist has represented the brickwork of the arches so as to obtain a purely ornamental effect—and this in a building where in fact brick is used in a particularly massive way.

Paintings in the western style are harmoniously combined with frames of carved Moorish woodwork in the famous reliquary triptych from the monastery of Piedra, preserved in the Academy of History, Madrid. Many other works—seats, cupboards, choir stalls, large chests—illustrate the high development of wood carving among the Mudejars. The carved doors and ceilings of Moorish buildings exerted a persistent influence in the Christian world. As late as 1633, at the height of the Baroque period, Diego López de Arenas wrote a treatise on woodwork in which he explained the technique of constructing Moorish ceilings.

The functional and the decorative are perfectly harmonized in these panelled and coffered ceilings. They were adapted to the slope of the roof at the sides, but flattened at the top. Inner and outer braces strengthened the wooden framework, which was decorated with ornamental marquetry and often with stucco pendants. Color and gold leaf were often added as well, making them exquisitely rich and beautiful. Most of the panelled ceilings that have survived in Spain date from the fifteenth and sixteenth centuries, although they were first used in Moorish buildings; this is proved by extensive remains of the original ceilings in the mosque of Cordova, while in Granada there are still such elaborate ceilings as the one in the Palace of Comares in the Alhambra.

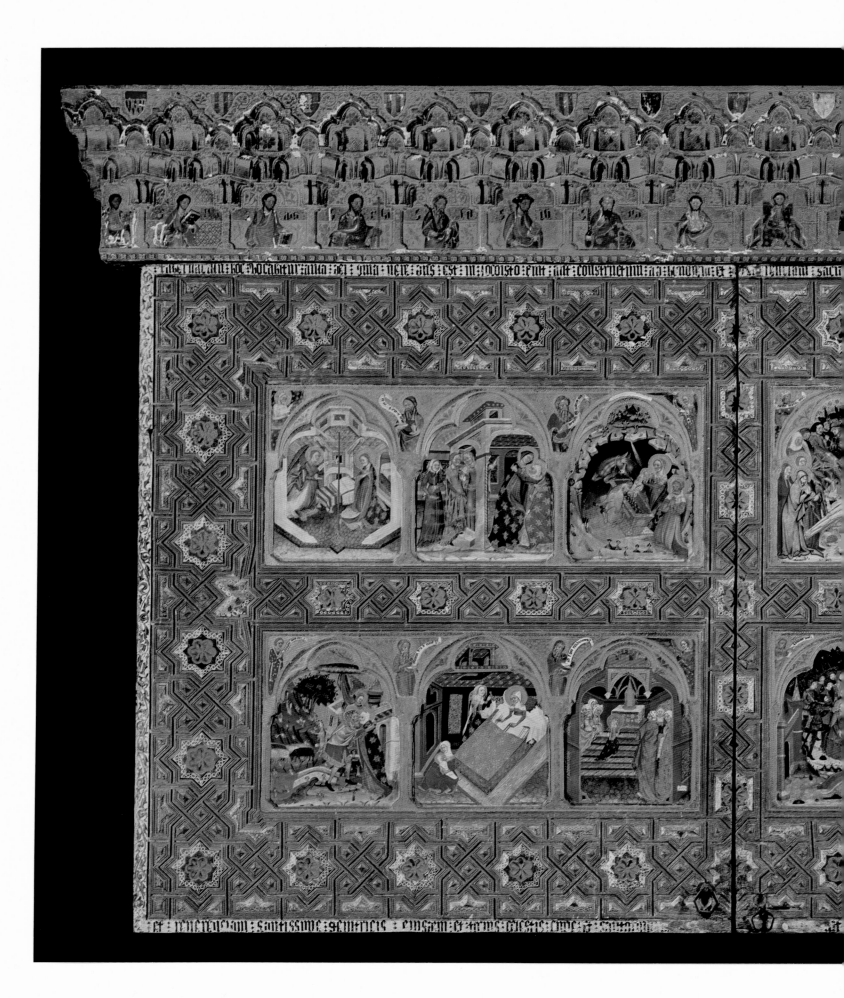

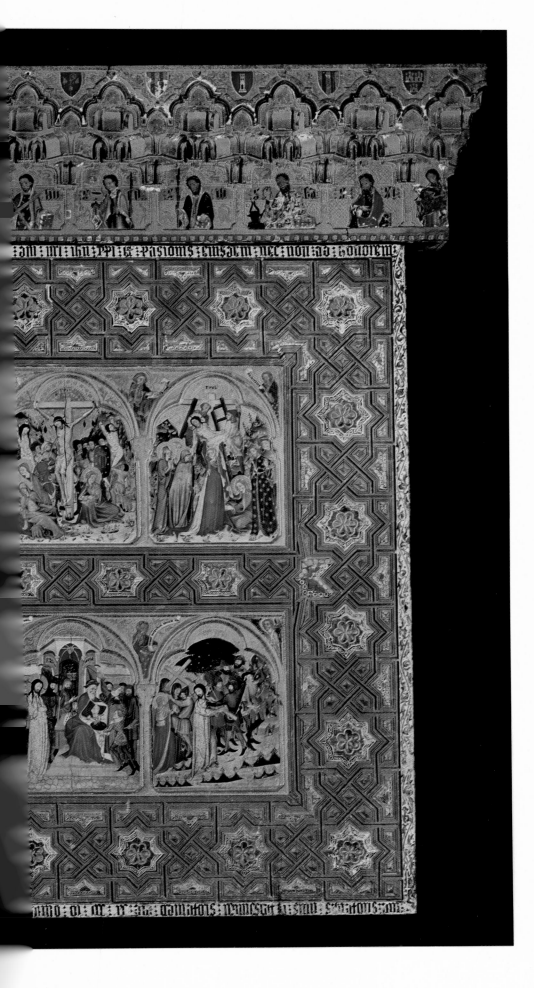

The reliquary triptych from the Monastery of Piedra, in Aragon, is one of the finest extant pieces of Moorish wood carving. The paintings framed by the woodwork are in the International Style and show above all the influence of the Serras, with reminiscences of the Sienese masters. When the folding doors are shut (as here), the front displays twelve scenes arranged in two rows, with episodes in the life of the Virgin and the Passion of Christ. In the spandrels of the arches framing these scenes are a number of separate figures. But the most interesting part of the triptych is the decorative pattern that surrounds the paintings: the knot motif, with eight-pointed stars, and the top edge with its profusion of ornament, stress the Orientalism of the whole. When the folding doors are open, we see the place prepared for the relics, with Gothic gables, and on the back of the doors are painted figures of angels playing musical instruments. An inscription records the date of the triptych: 1390.

RELIQUARY TRIPTYCH WITH MOORISH WOODWORK, FROM THE MONASTERY OF PIEDRA (SARAGOSSA). 1390. ROYAL ACADEMY OF HISTORY, MADRID.

MOORISH PANELLED CEILING. LATE 15TH CENTURY. SACRISTY OF THE CONVENT OF SAN FRANCISCO, PALENCIA.

Among many examples illustrating the wide variety of Moorish woodwork, the splendid panelled ceiling in the sacristy of San Francisco in Palencia testifies to the continuing vigor of Mudejar art in late fifteenth-century Spain. The ceiling of the large square room is divided into an octagon, and each of its eight coffered panels is decorated with solidly carved interlace patterns. The richest section of all is the central octagon at the top, with its gorgeous colors and a cluster of stucco pendants in the middle.

The woodwork, wall paintings, miniatures, stuccoes, ceramics, bronzes, ivories, textiles and jewelry illustrated here exemplify the fusion of styles that took place in medieval Spain. There East and West were reconciled, and in the world of art two ways of being and feeling met and mingled, to the enrichment of each.

SPAIN'S INTEGRATION
IN EUROPE

MASTER OF TAHULL: CHRIST IN MAJESTY. WALL PAINTING FROM SAN CLEMENTE DE TAHULL (LÉRIDA). 12TH CENTURY.
MUSEUM OF CATALAN ART, BARCELONA.

Many artistic forms of eastern origin found their way into Spain through the Moslems. But throughout the Middle Ages classical influences were also at work, as they had been in the ancient world. The Peninsula had been permeated by Greco-Roman culture, and in the end the Spanish peoples had become an integral part of the Roman world. By the time the Germanic invaders crossed the Pyrenees in the fifth century and spread all over the Peninsula, Spain had been so thoroughly romanized that, whatever the future might bring, she could never shake off this Roman influence.

While the Germanic peoples reigned in Spain, the classical spirit persisted. After the first wave of Suevi, Vandals and Alani came the Visigoths, who established themselves securely and ruled the country for three hundred years (during the fifth, sixth and seventh centuries), through an unbroken line of thirty-three kings. Once again the Goths showed that an invader with a lower culture than that of the people he conquers tends to be dominated by their higher civilization. Spain, like other countries of the Western Empire, did not lose everything the classical world had given her; indeed, for centuries there was a fruitful interchange between the life of conquered and conquerors. The Germanic peoples had no architectural traditions and none of the major arts; they brought into Spain only the minor arts, and a repertory of ornamental forms that were gradually fused with those of the classical tradition. And so the Middle Ages began, a thousand years considered by the men of the Renaissance as a period of unrelieved darkness and confusion. The Italian humanists spoke ingenuously of the "Gothic night" and took it for granted that everything done since the fall of the Roman Empire had been without exception the work of barbarians.

Today we know that the spirit of Rome survived throughout the Middle Ages and sometimes manifested itself vigorously. It is recognized now that a whole series of medieval "renaissances" took place: the Carolingian renaissance, the Ottonian renaissance, and then the rich flowering of the Romanesque period followed by the triumph of Gothic in the France of St Louis. Spain too had its "renaissances," by which it was made to feel that it shared the destiny of Europe.

SUN BETWEEN TWO ANGELS. RELIEF ON THE TRIUMPHAL ARCH, CHURCH OF QUINTANILLA DE LAS VIÑAS (BURGOS). 7TH-8TH CENTURY (?).

European art in the Middle Ages had a nostalgic longing for the ancient world, yet at the same time it was penetrated by Christian thought, which gave life a deeply religious meaning. The importance attached to Aristotle's ideas in medieval philosophy illustrates the hold of antiquity on men's minds. And so, for several centuries, there was an attempt to harmonize reason and faith. Yet, as medieval culture developed stage by stage, we can distinguish a continuous process of humanization, that is, an increasing emphasis on the values that exalt man as an individual, God's creature but also bound to the things of this world.

Owing to Spain's historical circumstances, its art was destined to play a decisive part in Europe's artistic development. Though it may seem paradoxical, it was through Andalusia that classical influences flowed back into Europe. The flourishing medieval school of translators in Toledo brought valuable books to the West; and in art, something similar happened. This was why the Iberian peninsula had an important place in the origins of two styles as strictly European as the Romanesque and the Gothic.

Political events led inexorably to the Reconquest, whose complex story cannot be told here. After the Moslem invasion, the Christians, starting from pockets of resistance in Asturias and Catalonia, advanced southwards—step by step, century by century. At first, people were probably unaware of the larger issues involved in the struggle. Before the year 1000, the wars between the Moslems and Christians were purely local; indeed, until the twelfth century the chroniclers seem to have had no idea of a lost Spain that must be recovered.

Within the Christian part of the country, however, from the eighth century to the tenth, the art of the early Middle Ages was trying, with varying degrees of intensity, to express itself in ways that might be called European, in reaction against those prevailing in the Moslem world. This is a tendency that must be borne in mind, after duly stressing the influence of the East on the whole of Spanish art, regardless of religious differences. In the later Middle Ages, during the Romanesque and Gothic periods, this tendency became much more marked. So, at the beginning of the fifteenth century, and particularly in the age of the Catholic Kings, Spain was in a state of great tension; but this did not prevent the final triumph of the Renaissance.

THE ROMAN AND THE ROMANESQUE

From the art of medieval Spain, what works and styles can be singled out which reflect the longing for a return to Rome ? A very careful analysis would mean studying the entire Middle Ages in the search for classical reminiscences. But for the purpose of this chapter we will stick to the periods between Early Christian and Gothic art.

For about seven centuries forms persisted that kept the spirit of Rome alive. The Visigoths copied classical building techniques. In the masonry of their churches they kept to the methods of Imperial times, and the lessons of Rome are found in their columns, piers and vaulting. Admittedly there are also horseshoe arches in Visigothic churches, with their suggestion of the East; but these were already known in the Latin world, and certainly did not prevent the survival of classicism.

Some early buildings in excellent condition have luckily survived in the Peninsula, and confirm this. There is the church of San Juan de Baños (Palencia), dated 661, whose plan and columns with Corinthian capitals recall Early Christian basilicas. The church of Santa Comba de Bande, in the mountainous province of Galicia, is very interesting in spite of its modest size; it has the plan of a Greek cross.

San Pedro de la Nave (Zamora), transferred from its original site a few years ago because the waters of a reservoir would otherwise have engulfed it, combines the basilical plan with the Greek cross. Like the other two buildings, it has ashlar masonry set in the Roman manner and is roofed with barrel vaults; it has semicircular arches and horseshoe arches, piers and columns, arcading in the transept and two rooms on each side of the chancel, with windows opening on to the main nave. The church of San Pedro de la Nave is as interesting architecturally as it is sculpturally. In an earlier chapter we stressed the Orientalism of the capitals and the mouldings; but its reliefs are a bridge between works in the Roman tradition and those that were later to come in the Romanesque period.

In the district of Campo de Lara, in the province of Burgos, the church of Quintanilla de las Viñas was discovered a few years ago. Although only part of the building has survived, its links with San Pedro de la Nave are extremely interesting. Both churches have been assigned to the Visigothic period; but this is probably too early a dating, and it seems likely that both were built after 711. If this is indeed so, then they show how Roman building techniques persisted in a part of Spain that had, practically speaking, remained free of the Moslems. At Quintanilla de las Viñas the solid walls of ashlar masonry are striking, and there are indications that the choir may have been roofed with a groined vault.

As for the decorations of the Quintanilla church, low reliefs are arranged in bands on the exterior; inside, they figure on the triumphal horseshoe arch, on the large imposts supporting it, and on several loose stones found out of place. The motifs are very varied and some of their themes were widespread in the classical world, though taken over and elaborated in Byzantine art. Stems rise up and curve out to form circles enclosing bunches of grapes and other plants; there are peacocks, too, and other birds, rosettes and even some letters that have so far not been interpreted unequivocally. Besides these motifs, there are reliefs showing Christ blessing and Christ between two angels, and allegories of the sun and moon. One of the latter is illustrated here: two winged figures, hovering in the air, hold up a disk containing a bust symbolizing the sun; it is inscribed SOL. These subjects, with the same meaning or with others, but similarly composed, are found on Roman triumphal arches and Byzantine ivories. The nearest parallel is the famous Barberini ivory in the Louvre.

The Roman background of Visigothic art is often modified by Byzantine influences. This has a special significance, as the Eastern Empire, like Spain, showed the crossing of two artistic trends, those developing within it, and those that came from Rome. The two ends of the Mediterranean, in fact, had similar experiences.

The development of Visigothic art suffered a harsh blow from the Moslem invasion in 711, for the influx of peoples from North Africa and the Middle East was to give an entirely new direction to the culture of the Peninsula. But, in spite of this, certain classical trends continued. The Moslems built their mosques, and took over Christian buildings: thus a hint of Rome persisted in Moorish art. The Moslems brought a new feeling for decoration; yet in Cordova, Toledo, Seville and other cities thoroughly "islamized," the lessons of the classical world were still apparent. The Great Mosque of Cordova, built on the site of a Visigothic church, retains elements taken from Roman works, and uses techniques taken from Imperial buildings.

It was in Asturias, the remote mountainous region of northern Spain, that the first reaction to the Moslem invasion appeared: there, in the eighth century, began what Spaniards call the Reconquista—the Reconquest. The first Christians who stood up to the Moslems cannot have realized what the struggle against the invaders meant. Rebellion began in a purely local way, simply to maintain a government that was independent of the Caliphate of Cordova.

After the battle of Covadonga (718), the first symbolic victory against the Moslems, the Christian kingdom of Asturias became more strongly knit. After hiding out in the mountain fastnesses, the Christians first established their court at Cangas de Onís, and finally Alfonso II the Chaste transferred the capital to the city of Oviedo. The king then sought to assert his power by undertaking a great building program. Alfonso erected several churches and near them a palace which, according to the chroniclers

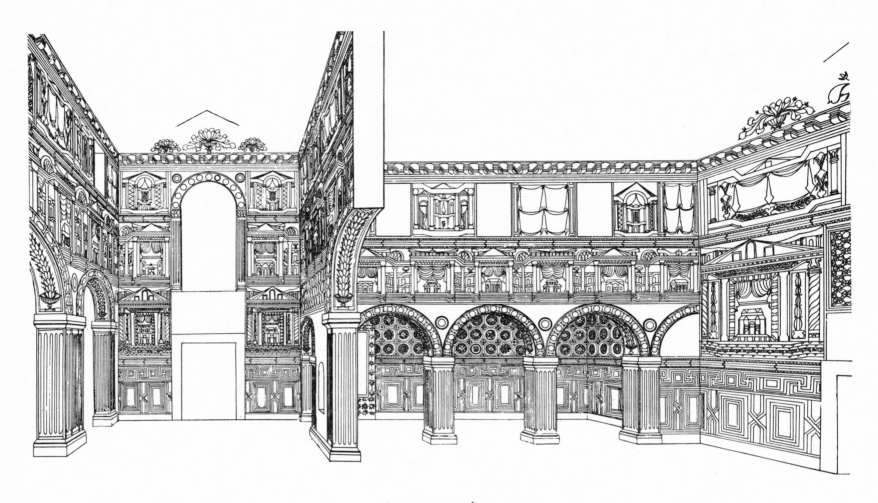

RECONSTRUCTION BY MAGÍN BERENGUER
OF THE WALL PAINTINGS IN THE CHURCH OF SAN JULIÁN DE LOS PRADOS (CALLED SANTULLANO), OVIEDO.

—and their accounts have been confirmed by excavations—was remarkably rich for its time. With its halls, towers, baths, and plumbing, it reveals the king's undoubted desire to imitate Roman refinements.

Of these early buildings in Oviedo, there are substantial remains only of the Cámara Santa and the churches of San Tirso and San Julián, generally called Santullano. The apse of the latter church is given a distinctive form by the arrangement of the chapels: a main one flanked by two side chapels, thus forming a tripartite apse which, though already known in Asturias itself, was to be imitated in a number of Spanish buildings elsewhere. These chapels were not semicircular at the back, as in other countries, but rectangular, thus departing from the basilical plan. This layout had appeared in some Syrian and Egyptian churches of the fifth and sixth centuries. Many Visigothic churches had a rectangular chancel, too, but without the tripartite apse found in Asturias.

Apart from these three vaulted chapels at the east end, the most notable features of the Santullano church are the return to the semicircular arch, the presence of a large transept, a three-aisled nave, porticoes, a room that must have been used as a sacristy and another room, above the main altar, that is very oddly planned because it has no means of communicating with the outside except through a window. The unusual proportions of each of its parts make the layout and design of this church very original; indeed, it is one of the most interesting Spanish buildings of the early Middle Ages.

The most attractive thing about Santullano is the paintings that once decorated it, enough of which remain to give us some idea of what they were like. The inside walls were covered with frescoes that immediately recall the styles of Pompeii, especially the so-called ornamental style, because they simulate buildings with slender columns and curtains, and in many cases make great play with perspective effects. The Santullano paintings have been ably restored by Magín Berenguer, and Professor Schlunk has pointed out the symbolism in their subjects. Their Roman background seems modified by the Christian spirit in which they are steeped, probably through Byzantine influences. Pictured in them are jewelled crosses of the kind that were first made by Spanish goldsmiths in the time of Alfonso III (866-909).

Architecture reached an even higher level in the reign of Ramiro I (842-850). For this, credit must go to an anonymous architect of exceptional ability, the so-called Master of Naranco, who by the use of new techniques succeeded in harmonizing the structural and the decorative. Half-way up Monte Naranco, which dominates the city of Oviedo, he built the palace—later a church, called Santa María de Naranco (see pp. 84-85)— that must have been used as a reception hall. It contains interesting ornamental motifs of Oriental origin, such as the stone disks with relief carvings that recall Sassanian works. From the structural point of view the palace of Naranco is exceptionally important too. An old chronicler described the admiration aroused by its barrel vaults reinforced with cross-ribs of Roman origin. It was no doubt the same architect who built the church of San Miguel de Lillo, a few hundred yards away from the palace.

The Master of Naranco's influence appears again in the church of Santa Cristina de Lena, which may have been built after the reign of Ramiro I by one of his pupils. It is a church of more modest proportions. From the rectangular nave project four smaller units: a chapel at the east end, the porch at the west end, and a room on each side. The walls are reinforced with buttresses which, considering the small size of the building, are quite unnecessary. But the most interesting and unusual features are found inside. The original iconostasis, dividing the altar and sanctuary from the rest of the church, is still in place: it consists of a row of columns with Corinthian capitals, supporting an arcade of semicircular arches. The carved closure slabs under the central arch, in front of the altar, are Visigothic work. These elements are the material remains of a liturgy that kept the officiating priest isolated from the congregation. This is still the practice in the eastern churches; in Spain it lasted until the eleventh century, when the Roman rites were introduced.

ICONOSTASIS IN THE CHURCH OF SANTA CRISTINA DE LENA AT VEGA DEL REY, NEAR OVIEDO (ASTURIAS). 9TH CENTURY.

All the developments of Asturian architecture were summed up in the church of San Salvador de Valdediós, built in 893 by Alfonso III the Great, who retired there when he was deposed by his sons. Within a plan that still recalls that of the Roman basilicas, it brings together various elements used in the buildings of Alfonso II and Ramiro I. The lofty nave is divided by piers into three aisles. As at Santullano, there is a room above the main altar at the east end. The nave is roofed with barrel vaults. Most remarkable of all is the presence of horseshoe arches in some of the windows, which seems to reflect the first influx of Mozarabic trends from the south. Some interesting remains of wall paintings are found in San Salvador, as in other churches in Asturias.

This fine group of Asturian churches illustrates the survival of classical traditions in northwestern Spain. Turning to Catalonia, in the northeastern part of the country, we find an equally interesting group of medieval churches: they are closely related to contemporary developments in the Romanesque architecture of Western Europe. Here the Pyrenees, far from being a barrier, formed a connecting link, and the Roussillon district in particular became a fruitful meeting-place between France and Spain.

Throughout the early Middle Ages classical elements appear in Catalan art, and the continuity between Visigothic work and work done after the Moslem invasion stands out clearly. In Catalonia it proved possible to reconcile local traditions with influences from both north and south: from Carolingian Europe on the one hand, and from the Islamic world on the other, through the important Mozarabic centers. These developments are summed up at Tarrasa, near Barcelona, in three churches standing in close proximity to one another, Santa María, San Miguel, and San Pedro. Another Catalan church, San Pedro de Roda, combining Mozarabic and classical influences, is the key building for an understanding of the forces which went to shape Catalan architecture in this crucial period of Western art.

Through the early medieval art of Asturias and Catalonia there runs a Roman strain which prevailed over other trends. This being so, Spain seemed marked out for a decisive role at one of the most important junctures in the history of European art—a juncture signalized by the rise of Romanesque. After the fall of the Roman Empire, which scattered the forces of the West, there was no unifying style of art in Europe until Romanesque emerged and made good. In the eastern half of the Empire, Byzantium produced an art with its own personality, wholly in the service of the eastern Church. In the West, under the domination of the Germanic peoples, styles appeared with features peculiar to each country. Thus a distinction has to be made at first between Merovingian architecture in France, Ostrogothic architecture in Italy, and Visigothic architecture in Spain. A few centuries later we have to distinguish between Carolingian, Lombard and Asturian art. But from about the year 1000 there arose an art that can rightly be described as European—the art we call Romanesque. Springing from a variety of influences, it developed into an international style, and so it cannot be considered narrowly, as the product of any one country. It originated not only in France, Italy, Spain or Byzantium, but was the outcome of a whole ferment of activities and influences in many parts of Europe.

Spain's historical circumstances at the time the Romanesque style took form had far-reaching effects on the course of art. The death of Al-Mansur in 1002 led to the break-up of the Caliphate of Cordova, and these events occurred at a providential moment. The Christian states found themselves in a strong position, thanks in particular to the leadership of a remarkable monarch in Navarre: Sancho the Great (1000-1035), whose long reign saw both territorial expansion and cultural advances. He united Castile and Aragon to his kingdom and made his influence felt in León and Catalonia. In an eleventh-century document he is described aptly enough as "King of the kings of Spain." His successors during the eleventh and twelfth centuries (when Romanesque was at its height) continued to advance southwards: Toledo was conquered in 1085, and Saragossa about 1118.

The outstanding personality in the cultural life of the period was a monk who, after taking orders in 1002 at the Catalan monastery of Ripoll, rose to become Bishop of Vich. His name was Oliva. He became the friend and adviser of Sancho the Great, and through him relations were established between Navarre and Catalonia. One of his pupils, Abbot Ponce, was appointed Bishop of Oviedo, in Asturias, and thus a network of religious connections was set up across the length and breadth of northern Spain. The relations between these Christian kingdoms were knit closer by the increasing flow of pilgrims through northern Spain along the road to Santiago de Compostela.

Several women in Sancho the Great's family appear to have been instrumental in the artistic revival that began with his reign, in the early years of the eleventh century, and continued without a pause. With this movement under way, Spain's incorporation into Europe was further hastened by a steady influx of peoples from beyond the Pyrenees who, together with the Mozarabs, helped to repopulate the country. For as the Christians gradually pushed southwards and reconquered the Moslem areas, the displaced Moslem population was replaced by Christian settlers. The great strength of the king's authority prevented the development here of a feudal system, such as had grown up in other European countries. But what was socially and artistically most important was the founding of many new towns in the expanding Christian kingdoms: these sprang up during the vast process of resettlement and repopulation, and for these new towns churches had to be built.

This accounts for the large number of Romanesque churches which now appeared in many parts of Spain. These circumstances, which have not hitherto been taken into account, go to explain many features of Spanish Romanesque, particularly the way it took root among the people in places as remote as Galicia.

VIEW OF THE CHURCH OF SAN SALVADOR DE VALDEDIÓS, NEAR OVIEDO (ASTURIAS). 893.

During the eleventh century, while Spain was thus changing—strengthening its ties with Europe, opening up its roads to pilgrims from France and elsewhere—it still maintained close contact with the Moslem world. Alfonso VI, who had reconquered Toledo from the Moors, took the title of "King of the Two Religions," perhaps on account of the ascendancy he gained over the Taifa kingdoms of Moorish Spain.

One of Alfonso's vassals was the Cid, the Spanish national hero, a real historical figure whose exploits are celebrated in *The Poem of the Cid*, an anonymous Castilian epic of the twelfth century. The Cid is an apparently contradictory personality. On the one hand he incarnates the virtues of the medieval Christian knight, loyal to his lord even when unjustly punished with exile; on the other, he is a typical "frontiersman,"

VIEW OF THE CHURCH OF SAN CLEMENTE, TAHULL (LÉRIDA). 12TH CENTURY.

NAVE OF THE CHURCH OF SAN VICENTE, CARDONA (BARCELONA). 10TH-11TH CENTURY.

who sees nothing wrong in being paid to serve the petty Moorish kings. The two attitudes can be reconciled in view of the long coexistence of peoples of different religions in Spanish history.

Throughout all the wars and rivalries, there may have arisen in the Romanesque period a higher ideal, one that could unite all those living in the Peninsula. The Christians had before them the idea of Reconquest, that is, of recovering the territory lost to the Moslems; and the idea of national unity, though still far away, was beginning to be felt; but the separation of Portugal, irrevocably turned into an independent kingdom, unfortunately began at the same time.

A nephew of the conqueror of Toledo, Alfonso VII (1126-1157), styled himself "Emperor of Spain," thus showing he sought power that would be recognized by every state in the Peninsula, whatever its language or religion. Unity was still far away, but at least the three great Christian kingdoms finally to be founded in the reign of the Catholic Kings were being built up: the kingdom of León and Castile, that of Aragon and Catalonia (united since 1162), and that of Navarre which, after its brilliant beginning, remained isolated and without any chance of expanding.

Such, in outline, is the historical background. Something may now be said about the part played by Spain in the rise of Romanesque architecture. The Spanish contribution to the new style was made through three distinct currents of influence.

The first arose in Asturias where, as early as the ninth century, we find buildings stemming directly from the Roman tradition, like the group of churches in or near Oviedo built by Alfonso II and Ramiro I. Santa María de Naranco might also be described as Romanesque. The second current was of Oriental origin: Mozarabic art contributed to Romanesque chiefly in the field of decoration, though in some cases it preserved and transmitted certain classical elements.

The third current of Spanish influence, and one that had a decisive impact on the development of Romanesque, came from Catalonia and Roussillon. This area lies astride the Pyrenees, and its Romanesque churches, whether located on the French or the Spanish side of the frontier, have an essential unity of style. Some of them date to the last years of the tenth century, some to the early decades of the eleventh. Mozarabic influence here is equally evident in the churches of Spanish Catalonia and in those of French Roussillon like Saint-Michel de Cuxa and Saint-Genis des Fontaines. All alike represent what J. Puig y Cadafalch has described as the "first Romanesque art." It can be seen taking form in some highly interesting Catalan churches of very early date, like San Clemente de Tahull, San Vicente de Cardona and the abbey church of Ripoll; they sometimes reveal imported features such as the rows of small round arches, of Lombard origin, decorating apses and towers.

Asturian, Mozarabic and Catalan art of the ninth, tenth and eleventh centuries played a vital role in the development of European Romanesque. But to achieve a fruitful exchange between Spain and the rest of Europe—for Spanish work to be known outside Spain, for European work to be assimilated within the Peninsula—something else was needed. Romanesque might never have achieved its international position without the interchange of artists and ideas that took place through pilgrimages.

For Romanesque was a style that developed owing to the way in which Christians moved from place to place and from country to country, sometimes as soldiers, sometimes as pilgrims, and, most fruitfully of all, as artists. In its essentials, Romanesque may be described as a synthesis of the art of Rome and that of various Eastern cultures—a synthesis first fused with a whole series of local traditions, and then gradually internationalized as the relations between different countries grew closer. In all these cross-currents, pilgrims to the tomb of St Peter in Rome, to the Holy Places in Palestine and, in particular, to Santiago de Compostela from the middle of the tenth century on, played an important part.

In the time of Alfonso II (791-842), the great promoter of Asturian art, a "marble chest" was miraculously discovered at Compostela, in the heart of Galicia. The remains in it were identified as those of the apostle St James the Great. News of the discovery quickly spread among Christian peoples of the West, and in the year 950 the first pilgrim whose name we know, Godescalc, made his way to Compostela. Thereafter the flow of pilgrims never ceased, except perhaps during Al-Mansur's devastating raids into Christian territory. By many roads and even by sea people flocked to venerate the shrine of St James, and gradually the pilgrimage was organized through the setting up of hospices and monasteries along the various routes. The great Benedictine abbey of Cluny, in Burgundy, played a decisive part in the promotion of these journeys, and Cluniac foundations multiplied all over northern Spain under the protection of the kings of Navarre, Castile and León. To Christians, Compostela became rather what Mecca was to Moslems, and the figure of St James came to represent a kind of anti-Mohammed. The crusades, turning eastward, and also playing an important part in the development of Romanesque, had their counterpart in the West.

Spanish Romanesque art owes its distinctive characteristics to the pilgrimage road to Compostela. Over that road ideas made their way as well as travellers, thus bringing about the decisive fusion of the Hispanic and the European. Eastern influences were still at work, as we have seen, right up to the time of the Catholic Kings, but it was only from the eleventh century on that Spain really declared itself a Western country. After the early bursts of artistic activity that produced the first Romanesque churches of León (deriving from Asturian architecture) and Catalonia, came a much more mature and international style, which took definite shape in Santiago de Compostela. This is the style that might be fittingly called "pilgrimage Romanesque."

RECONSTRUCTION BY K. J. CONANT OF THE ROMANESQUE CATHEDRAL OF SANTIAGO DE COMPOSTELA.
INSTITUTO PADRE SARMIENTO DE ESTUDIOS GALLEGOS, SANTIAGO DE COMPOSTELA.

The earliest Romanesque monuments in the kingdom of León are the crypt of San Antolín at Palencia and the porch of San Isidoro in the city of León; the structure of the latter is of Asturian origin, but the capitals are Mozarabic. The finest piece of Romanesque architecture in Catalonia must have been the great Abbey of Ripoll, rebuilt by Oliva and consecrated in 1032. It was completely renovated, unfortunately, in the nineteenth century, and much of its value was then lost.

The Catalan church of San Vicente de Cardona, on the other hand, has kept much of its original form in spite of later additions; it has three apses of semicircular plan, a transept and a three-aisled nave, and the series of small round arches that decorate the outside walls are proof of Lombard influence on early Catalan Romanesque.

Pilgrimage Romanesque is represented along the road to Compostela by four outstanding monuments. The first is the cathedral of Jaca, which the researches of Ubieto have shown to be later in date than once was thought. It has a noble simplicity of design: its plan is basilical, with a three-aisled nave in which piers and columns alternate, and three semicircular apses. The second, probably deriving from Jaca cathedral, is San Martín de Frómista. This may be considered the perfect archetype of the Romanesque church, with its harmonious organization of space and its aisles divided only by piers with engaged shafts. The third is the new church of San Isidoro in León, with a cruciform plan. Fourth and last is the cathedral of Santiago de Compostela, which brings to fruition all the skills and techniques acquired by the early Romanesque church-builders both in Spain and elsewhere.

CLOISTER OF THE MONASTERY OF SANTO DOMINGO DE SILOS (BURGOS). 11TH-12TH CENTURY.

PLATERIAS MASTER: THE WOMAN TAKEN IN ADULTERY. EARLY 12TH CENTURY.
RELIEF ON THE PORTADA DE PLATERIAS, CATHEDRAL OF SANTIAGO DE COMPOSTELA.

Begun about 1075 by Bishop Diego Peláez, the great basilica of Compostela must have been nearly finished (except perhaps for the main façade) by 1122, in the time of Archbishop Diego Gelmírez. Although externally the cathedral has undergone many later changes, the interior has come down to us almost intact. Plan and elevation go to form a harmonious whole. It is a cruciform church with a three-aisled nave, a three-aisled transept, and an ambulatory with nine apsidal chapels. Over the side aisles a gallery runs along the whole length of the church. The vaulting is varied to suit each part of the structure: over the central aisle of the nave is a cross-ribbed barrel vault, whose thrust is absorbed by the quadrant-vaulted galleries, while the side aisles are covered by groined vaults. The interior is beautifully proportioned throughout—in the arrangement of arches, the span of the bays, and the general organization of space. Here, it would seem, were raised and solved all those problems that were later to obsess Renaissance architects, who thought of a building as the outcome of a complex system of rhythms and mathematical calculations. Santiago cathedral shows an abiding sense of classical equilibrium and proportions, thus testifying to that strong attachment to the Roman tradition which underlies Romanesque architecture.

What church, or churches, was it that supplied the model for the general plan and type of structure exemplified at Santiago de Compostela? This is still a matter of controversy. Suffice it to say that in France there is a whole series of pilgrimage churches which undoubtedly antedate Santiago cathedral and must be considered in any analysis of it. Among them are Saint-Martin at Tours, Saint-Martial at Limoges, Saint-Remi at Rheims, Sainte-Foy at Conques and Saint-Sernin at Toulouse. Something of what the pilgrimage route meant in actual practice is shown in the case of an artist who left his mark in several widely scattered places. Since his finest work is on the Portada de las Platerías, the portal of the south transept of Santiago cathedral, let us call him the Platerías Master. Among sculptures by several different hands, his stand out because of their sensitive relief carving, the modelling of drapery, and the expression and personality he gives every one of his figures. All these characteristics are found in the Woman taken in Adultery, on one of the tympana.

The pilgrims' guide book, the twelfth-century Codex Calixtinus, gives a description of this south portal of Santiago cathedral: "We must not forget that beside the temptation of Our Lord is a woman holding the putrefying head of her lover, which her husband cut off and forced her to kiss twice a day. Oh, what a terrible and wonderful punishment for the woman taken in adultery, and what a lesson for all who see it!" The vigorous, expressionistic style of this figure reappears in others, presumably also the work of the Platerías Master, not only in the same portal but also in the Puerta del Pardón of San Isidoro at León, in some fragmentary sculptures from the vanished Romanesque cathedral of Pamplona, and in some reliefs in Saint-Sernin at Toulouse. Here is strong evidence that artists moved freely from place to place, working wherever there was employment, regardless of frontiers.

A little off the road to Santiago, but still in the style of pilgrimage Romanesque, is the cloister of Santo Domingo de Silos (Burgos), one of the most beautiful and complete to come down to us from this period. A large number of extraordinarily interesting capitals decorate the arcades on its two storeys, and eight reliefs stand at the corners of the lower cloister. The capitals are grouped two by two, and, like the reliefs, are the work of several hands. The carving of one capital, which must be the oldest, shows a technique akin to that of the Cordova ivories: birds and hybrid animals, surrounded by stalks, are modelled with wonderful skill. The idea of the composition is wholly Moorish, and the care lavished on the smallest detail recalls the techniques of ivory carving. Whether there is any particular symbolism in these sculptures or not, they are chiefly remarkable for the use of decorative motifs whose point is purely ornamental. Other capitals have scenes with figures: some of the subjects are secular, but most of them illustrate events from the Gospels. In some cases (for instance, the Entombment of Christ or Doubting Thomas) these historiated capitals are closely related to the pilgrimage style, as can be seen by comparing them with the capitals in the cloister of Moissac in southwestern France.

From the eleventh century on, the Christian West began to revive an art form that had been abandoned since classical times: large-scale relief sculpture. This became a prominent feature in the decoration of Romanesque churches. It is instructive to follow the development of this figure sculpture from the earliest attempts, such as the reliefs, dated 1020, above the doorway of Saint-Genis des Fontaines, in Roussillon, to the great tympana of the twelfth-century churches. But the importance of these monumental relief sculptures does nothing to lessen the interest of smaller works.

The capitals at Silos serve to remind us of the important part played by the workshops of ivory-carvers in maintaining the traditions of figure carving. The ivory panels of the casket of the Beatitudes, from León, now in the National Archaeological Museum, Madrid, illustrate the trend towards strictly Romanesque forms. This small chest may well be the work of a pupil of the artist who carved the casket of San Isidoro;

ALTAR FRONTAL FROM THE MONASTERY OF SANTO DOMINGO DE SILOS (BURGOS). GILT COPPER INLAID WITH ENAMELS. EARLY 12TH CENTURY. PROVINCIAL MUSEUM, BURGOS.

THE BATLLÓ CHRIST, FROM OLOT (GERONA). POLYCHROME WOOD. MID-12TH CENTURY. MUSEUM OF CATALAN ART, BARCELONA.

DESCENT FROM THE CROSS, FROM ERILL-LA-VALL (LÉRIDA). WOOD. SECOND HALF OF THE 12TH CENTURY.
EPISCOPAL MUSEUM, VICH (BARCELONA).

THE ANNUNCIATION TO THE SHEPHERDS. LAST THIRD OF THE 12TH CENTURY.
FRESCO IN THE PANTEÓN DE LOS REYES, CHURCH OF SAN ISIDORO, LEÓN.

but no horseshoe arches appear in its reliefs, although there is a profusion of architectural motifs. The composition of its figures, which are handled more freely than hitherto, shows a desire to break away from the Byzantine rigidity which is so marked a feature of earlier Leonese works.

An altar frontal from the monastery of Silos, now in the museum at Burgos, is even more closely connected with art trends beyond the Pyrenees. It is a magnificent piece of metalwork, enriched with enamels like those of Limoges. On the front, enclosed in the mystical almond-shaped aureole called the mandorla, is the seated figure of Christ. Spaced out on either side are the Apostles framed in a series of arches with buildings above them—rather like what we saw in the reliefs on the ivory casket of the Beatitudes. The most remarkable thing about it is the figures, whose heads are colored with enamels. Whether the Burgos frontal was made by a Spanish artist or imported from France is not known, but in either case it shows how readily styles were transmitted along the pilgrimage road and diffused far beyond their place of origin.

MASTER OF MADERUELO: THE CREATION OF ADAM AND THE TEMPTATION. 12TH CENTURY.
FRESCO FROM THE HERMITAGE OF VERA CRUZ AT MADERUELO (SEGOVIA). PRADO, MADRID.

Another important and influential art form was free-standing sculpture, and it was now, in Romanesque Spain, that polychrome statuary was introduced into churches and began that long evolution which reached its height in the sixteenth and seventeenth centuries. These painted statues were produced all over the northern half of the Peninsula, but the main workshops were in Catalonia. Certain iconographical types were most common, and the Virgin and Child group is the most characteristic. The pose of the figures is strongly hieratic, following the Byzantine tradition: Mary is not presented as a mother, but as the throne of God, seated stiffly and holding the Child, who is solemnly blessing. One of the most representative of these polychrome figures is the Batlló Christ, carved in wood. Other magnificent examples, in stone, are the Virgins of Sahagún and Solsona, or, in wood covered with metal, enamelling or jewels, the Virgin of La Vega in Salamanca and the Sagrario Virgin in Toledo.

Color in sculpture leads on to color in manuscript illuminations, murals and panel paintings. In these three fields Spanish Romanesque is especially rich. Miniatures developed excitingly from the days of the Mozarabic Beatus manuscripts, the composition tending to become freer and more naturalistic, and sometimes foreshadowing Gothic. Two twelfth-century examples illustrate the change of style that had taken place. The first may be considered the finest illuminated manuscript of its kind from this period: the *Libro de los Testamentos*, or cartulary, of Oviedo cathedral. Symmetry is all-important in its compositions; elongated and highly expressive, the figures are framed with decorative motifs of very mixed origin that heighten the monumental air of the illustrations; and the feeling for calligraphy and color is strong, the colors being very skillfully combined.

The *Libro de los Testamentos* can be assigned to the first third of the twelfth century. The Avila Bible, now in the National Library in Madrid, dates to the end of the century. It lacks the elegance of the Oviedo manuscript; instead, it has a hectic sense of movement, with the figures all twisted and distorted, sometimes violently so. Before Gothic gave a new spirit to art, the Romanesque miniature was filled with expressionist feeling.

Romanesque mural painting is of particular interest, the more so since very little that is earlier than the eleventh century has reached us. What is left from Roman and early Christian times is very meagre. Thanks to the studies of Professor Schlunk, and the work of the restorer Magín Berenguer, the frescoes that once decorated Asturian churches have been brilliantly reconstructed. To these works also belong the frescoes from the Mozarabic church of San Baudel de Berlanga (Soria), with figures of animals and warriors that appear to be wholly secular, devoid of any religious associations. But all these are isolated works; none of them form an ordered sequence, as is usually the case with Romanesque wall paintings.

Wall painting in Romanesque Spain begins with the apse decorations in the Pyrenean churches of Catalonia and Aragon. Most of these frescoes long remained hidden from view behind Baroque altars. Nearly all of them have now been detached and transferred to museums, in particular to the Museum of Catalan Art in Barcelona. We can trace in them the work of masters and schools whose influence spread as far as the Castilian plateau. Both the themes and the composition of these apse paintings are usually of Byzantine origin. A good example is that of San Clemente de Tahull: in the semidome of the apse, enclosed in the mandorla, is the figure of Christ in Majesty, with the stars and other symbols from the Apocalypse around it, and the feet resting on the globe of the world. On the concave wall that sustains the vault, stand the apostles, stiffly, divided by columns. In the background are strips of color that suggest sky and earth.

Closely related to the art of Tahull are the paintings that decorated the hermitage of Vera Cruz at Maderuelo, in Castile (province of Segovia). Some years ago they were removed and taken to the Prado, as the church was about to be engulfed in a reservoir. The walls and barrel vaults of this small rectangular church must have been completely covered with Biblical scenes. The vault was occupied by Christ in Majesty, with angels in the corners; at the end was the Lamb as victim, and along the lower parts of the walls was a series of figures from the Old and New Testaments, with Adam and Eve next to the Twelve Apostles. Scenes and figures so dissimilar can seldom have been grouped together, and some are especially interesting because highly unusual: the scene of the creation of Adam, for instance, and that of the Temptation, both show a primitive feeling for landscape in the trees, with their strangely twisted branches. The naked figures of Adam and Eve are interesting, too, for their anatomical details, unsophisticatedly painted, but with a good deal of plastic vigor.

Tahull and Maderuelo belong to the first third of the twelfth century; their art reached its final development in the vaults of the Panteón de los Reyes (Royal Pantheon) of San Isidoro in León. Here is Castilian painting on a large scale, grouping a wide variety of themes, with a vitality and freedom in the composition that are far removed from the Byzantine world. Admittedly the figure of Christ in Majesty is still there, within the mandorla and surrounded by the symbols of the four Evangelists. But there are other subjects full of narrative vigor. In the Last Supper the attitudes of the figures are very varied and the objects on the table are carefully delineated. The

ALTAR FRONTAL WITH THE VIRGIN AND CHILD AND SCENES FROM THE LIFE OF ST MARGARET. FROM THE MONASTERY OF SANT MARTÍ SESCORTS (BARCELONA). 12TH CENTURY. EPISCOPAL MUSEUM, VICH (BARCELONA).

ALTAR FRONTAL WITH ST JOHN THE BAPTIST, FROM GESERA (HUESCA). 13TH CENTURY. MUSEUM OF CATALAN ART, BARCELONA.

Massacre of the Innocents has great plastic strength, with its groups of figures framed within a series of arches. The Annunciation to the Shepherds is dynamic and convincingly realistic: goats are climbing up to nibble leaves off the trees, a shepherd gives milk to one of the dogs, another turns towards the messenger of God. The figures and animals are cleverly arranged on the curving surface of a groined vault, so that they can be looked at from various angles.

Finally, Romanesque painting in Spain appears in one other form: the painted wooden panels of altar frontals. Out of these extremely interesting works there developed in time the painted altarpiece, which became increasingly important in Spanish art of the later Middle Ages. Panel painting at this time, however, was a typically Catalan art form and hardly existed outside Catalonia, where it was carried on in workshops that reached their highest stage of development in the twelfth century in such places as La Seo de Urgel, Vich and Ripoll.

ALTAR FRONTAL FROM SORIGUEROLA (GERONA). LA

The altar frontal from the church of Soriguerola (Gerona), preserved in the Museum of Catalan Art, Barcelona, is the masterpiece of an artist whose style exemplifies the transition, now well under way, towards Gothic art. Indeed this frontal may be said to mark the end of Romanesque panel painting. Its composition departs from the rigid layout that had prevailed up to now, and the picture space is enlarged or reduced according to the demands of the subject and the painter's whim. A vertical band, decorated with stems and leaves, runs down the middle of the frontal, dividing the subjects grouped on either side into two horizontal zones.

CENTURY. MUSEUM OF CATALAN ART, BARCELONA.

The imagery of the Soriguerola frontal consists of contrasting themes with no logical connection between them. On the left side, the whole of the lower register is taken up with the Last Supper. The upper register, with rows of trefoil arches, and the square frames on the right, contain scenes from the story of St Michael. Outstanding are those in which the archangel is seen weighing souls on Mount Gargano and fighting the dragon. There are also some seated figures of kings (representing the blessed perhaps) and a group of devils in hell. The style of the whole work is strongly expressionistic, with vigorous drawing and vividly contrasting colors.

The altar frontal came into existence as the conception of the altar changed and developed. In earlier times the altar had been a very simple, table-shaped affair, consisting nearly always of a mere central support with a stone slab on top of it. As the priests celebrated Mass facing the congregation, the front of the table began to be decorated with painted scenes, very similar to those in mural paintings. In the center was the enthroned figure of Christ in Majesty, enclosed in the mystical almond-shaped aureole or mandorla, and surrounded by the symbols of the four Evangelists. On either side and generally arranged on two registers, one above the other, were the figures of the Apostles or scenes from the Gospels. Other altar frontals represented the Virgin Mary or various saints with scenes from their lives.

The large number of altar frontals that have been preserved span a period of considerably more than a century, from the beginning of the twelfth century until well into the thirteenth. They represent a remarkably varied group of paintings. Some are conceived in a distinctly archaic style, while others already give a foretaste of Gothic art. In view of the importance attaching to these Catalan altar frontals as precursors of the great Spanish altar paintings of later times, we may pause here to consider two panels of the thirteenth century—characteristic examples of the robust vitality of this art, with its ever-present tendency towards expressionism.

The frontal dedicated to St John the Baptist in the Museum of Catalan Art in Barcelona was made in an unidentified workshop by a master carried away by his inspiration: the result is an appealing blend of naïveté and realism. The central figure of the saint, standing with his right hand raised, his right side and shoulder bare, and a book resting against his left knee, is inspired by the type-figure of Christ in Majesty. In the background is the schematized outline of a tree, its branches jutting out around the saint in a series of pear-shaped tufts. But in spite of all that is archaic about it, the figure is an arresting presence, with its large staring eyes and tousled hair outlined against the halo. On either side of the Baptist, arranged on three registers, are animals (in pairs, on the two lower levels) and two groups of figures who appear to be listening to the voice of the saint, "preaching in the wilderness." The animals—an eagle, a winged quadruped, a bull, a kind of dog, a lion, a bear, a deer and a wild boar—recall those in the Beatus manuscripts: it would seem that these are the animals of Noah's Ark. The human figures, above them, have an unruffled ease of movement which relates them to the new spirit of Gothic art. Much more advanced stylistically, and of higher artistic quality too, is the frontal from Soriguerola (Gerona), which is reproduced and described on pages 160-161.

THE NEW SPIRIT OF FORMS

The European currents that developed so actively in Spain during the eleventh and twelfth centuries, owing in particular to the pilgrimage road to Santiago de Compostela, continued in the centuries that followed without a break until our own time. But from the end of the twelfth century things changed; after that, in the exchange of forms and artists, Spain was to take very much more, and to give out very much less. Yet, thanks to the vitality of eastern influences, right up to the end of the Middle Ages it maintained its own distinctive presence and personality.

The fact that Spain was now closely involved in European problems explains the importance in Spanish art of the transition from Romanesque to Gothic. Political, social, economic, and in particular religious factors all played a part in this gradual change-over from one style to another. Politically, throughout the twelfth century, the Christian kings of northern Spain predominated over the Moslems. Alfonso VI dared to call himself "King of the Two Religions" but his nephew Alfonso VII styled himself "Imperator totius Hispaniae," Emperor of all Spain. The ideal of unity, which was to be achieved in the last years of the fifteenth century, with the Catholic Kings, had been born, and was maintained, in spite of recurrent political crises.

At the beginning of the thirteenth century, some momentous events took place: the kingdom of Castile and León (united for good by Ferdinand III the Holy) extended its boundaries into Andalusia, so that the entire valley of the Guadalquivir, with the great cities of Cordova and Seville, was brought under Christian rule. The eastern states (Aragon and Catalonia) also gained new territory at the expense of the Moslems, when James I conquered Valencia and Majorca. By the end of the thirteenth century, in fact, the map of Spain was pretty well settled as it would be until the time of the Catholic Kings. The crown of Castile held sway southwards as far as the kingdom of Granada, which held out until 1492. The crown of Aragon extended as far as Murcia, where its frontier with Castile had been established. In the shadow of the Pyrenees, the kingdom of Navarre maintained its independence until 1512, when it was annexed to the other kingdoms of Spain by Ferdinand the Catholic.

As the Middle Ages advanced, the social and economic life of Spain underwent far-reaching changes. Most important of all was probably the growth of the towns. Livestock-rearing increased in Old Castile and wool was exported in large quantities to the weavers established in Flanders. In the kingdom of Aragon the development of town life, agriculture and industry was combined with a thriving overseas trade. Catalan ships sailed the Mediterranean as far as Greece, and Valencia, Barcelona and Palma were very active ports in the last centuries of the Middle Ages.

The kingdom of Granada played a very important part in Spanish life during the thirteenth, fourteenth and fifteenth centuries. Its cities lived on the agricultural wealth of the wide plains around them. But apart from these forms of inland economy, there were others, like the silk industry, which faced outwards and linked many countries of the Moslem East by trade with the Christian kingdoms. It may have been these industries and trade relations that enabled the Moorish kingdom of Granada to survive until the end of the Middle Ages, when a radical change took place in the economic structure of these eastern countries.

Profound changes were also taking place in religious life. The negative, pessimistic sense of life that had been dominant in the early Middle Ages was giving way to a different mood. Life, in all that was written during the Romanesque age, seemed closely bound to sin, perfection could not be found except outside the world, in a monastery, far from passion and temptation, and God was a very long way from sorrowing humanity. In Romanesque imagery the figure of Christ was hieratic, and far removed from the faithful. This idea of God and man was strengthened in the first half of the twelfth century by the religious reform of St Bernard, who strictly enforced the separation of the monk from the world. Cistercian monasteries were accordingly built in remote places. Yet St Bernard's reform brought about a strange paradox. Though ignorant in matters of art, he was responsible for decisive changes in monastic architecture through the negative attitude he adopted. He condemned sculpture and decoration in churches and cloisters as tending to distract the monks. He wished to see churches built soberly, with simple structures in which he preferred new elements such as the pointed arch and cross-vaults. Thus there arose what may be described as Cistercian art: it bridged this period of transition and had unexpected results in Spain.

But it was not really St Bernard's activity that gave a new spirit to forms. Other monks felt themselves close to the things of this world and found a much warmer response among the faithful. The most extraordinary case is that of Suger, abbot of Saint-Denis, near Paris. His rebuilding of the abbey church of Saint-Denis was one of the greatest events in the history of art. There, Gothic art, which was making its first timid appearance in the Cistercian churches, was decisively affirmed. The porch and choir of Saint-Denis pointed the way for the building of the great Gothic cathedrals. Together with its pointed arches and rib-vaults, it included stained-glass windows, flying buttresses, and figure sculptures steeped in a new sense of humanity. It was thus that Suger interpreted the spirit of his time.

Without bearing all this in mind it is impossible to understand the change that took place in Spain, where the transition style developed in two ways. Cistercian art spread over the whole Peninsula, and its influence may explain the characteristic sobriety of Gothic churches in Aragon. But it is the impact of the abbey of Saint-Denis that explains the change of spirit which came over the art of Castile.

In the second half of the twelfth century and the first half of the thirteenth, Cistercian architecture in Spain produced a number of monasteries that were not only remarkably simple in design but remarkably large. First of all came Moreruela, in the province of Zamora, which typifies the transition from Romanesque to Gothic forms; it combines thick walls and semicircular arches with rib-vaults and pointed arches. The ruins of Moreruela show the beginning of a style that spread with unusual rapidity during the last third of the twelfth century. In all the medieval Christian kingdoms of northern Spain there are magnificent examples of Cistercian architecture: Osera, Oya, Meira, Armenteira, and Melón in Galicia; Palazuelos, La Espina, Santa María de Huerta, and Las Huelgas in Castile; Fitero and La Oliva in Navarre; Santas Creus and Poblet in Catalonia. The cycle of monastic art thus came to a close. In other countries the Cistercian style seemed a kind of blind alley, but in Spain its spirit survives in the cathedrals of Catalonia, Valencia and Palma (Majorca).

The art of Abbot Suger of Saint-Denis found its most brilliant manifestation in Spain in the Portico de la Gloria of the cathedral of Santiago de Compostela, the work of an artist whose name we know and who left a great deal of work behind him—Master Mateo. According to the French art-historian Henri Focillon, the spiritual dynasty founded by this great sculptor continued through Claus Sluter and survived to our own time through Michelangelo and Rodin; and certainly a new, vibrant way of

MASTER MATEO: THE PROPHET DANIEL. 1168-1188. SCULPTURE IN THE PORTICO DE LA GLORIA, CATHEDRAL OF SANTIAGO DE COMPOSTELA.

DOORWAY OF THE CHURCH OF SAN VICENTE, ÁVILA. LATE 12TH CENTURY.

CHURCH OF SAN VICENTE, ÁVILA: RELIEF ON THE CENOTAPH OF THE HOLY MARTYRS. LATE 12TH CENTURY.

envisaging the human spirit is evident in the Portico de la Gloria at Compostela. The sculptured figures in the tympana, arches and columns broke away from the hieratic solemnity of Romanesque and spoke directly to the faithful. They express a more optimistic view of life: the figure of Daniel appears smiling, as if freed of the dramatic forebodings that dominated Christian art in the centuries before it.

This new ease of expression was based on a new sense of form. The figures lost their traditional stiffness and turned towards one another, as if conversing: the group of the twenty-four Elders decorating the central arch, or the column-statues of the Apostles and Prophets, have an intense feeling of movement. The figures stand at various levels, composed with great naturalism; some seem to be speaking to those in front of them—and the faithful even came to imagine what they were saying. On the pilgrims who flocked to Compostela, the effect of all this must have been very strong. In its style and imagery, as well as in its warm expression of human values, the Portico de la Gloria is closely related to the art of Saint-Denis. We shall never know whether Master Mateo was born in Spain or elsewhere, but he was certainly well acquainted with what was going on in France and in particular with the work of Abbot Suger. In one of the arches of the Portico he represented the damned and the elect just as they were in the porch of Saint-Denis; the iconography of the tympanum, with Christ the Judge pointing to his wounds, answers to a new conception of art that had spread from Saint-Denis; the figure of the Judge has lost much of the hieratic solemnity it had in Romanesque sculpture and painting. The apocalyptic symbols are shown together with the instruments of the Passion: cross, crown of thorns, nails, etc.

With Master Mateo we come for the first time in the Middle Ages to an artist with a strong, self-assertive personality, quite as conscious of his powers as the great artists of the Renaissance. He not only inscribed his name on the lintels of the Portico (set up in 1188), proudly recording the fact that he directed the work from its inception, but also left a portrait of himself in a kneeling figure looking towards the high altar.

A new age in the history of Spanish art thus began, in architecture as well as sculpture, for the Portico de la Gloria is one of the first works in Spain (possibly even earlier than the Cistercian monasteries) in which we find pointed arches and rib-vaults.

As an artist, Master Mateo was certainly schooled in the West and his work keeps firmly to the main line of the European tradition. Yet like so many other artists he felt and responded to the appeal of Moslem art. The cusped arches, horseshoe arches, and ornamental motifs he used show his predilection for decorative elements that first appeared in the Great Mosque of Cordova.

The new spirit of forms is also revealed in some outstanding works by other Spanish sculptors towards the end of the twelfth century. In the group of Apostles in the Cámara Santa of Oviedo cathedral and in the portal and cenotaph of the church of San Vicente at Ávila, there is the same sense of unimpeded movement and the same effort to relate figures to each other. Whether these sculptures are earlier or later than Mateo's work is a complex problem, but there can be no doubt of their great artistic value; they testify to the high level of excellence attained by the transitional style in Spain. In the portal of San Vicente at Ávila, the freely flowing draperies of the column figures have been admirably rendered. In the cenotaph reliefs, dedicated to St Vincent and his sisters St Sabina and St Cristeta, the story of their persecution and martyrdom is told with refined and delicate touches.

Spanish Gothic made its appearance during the second half of the twelfth century in some outstanding works which, without diverging from the main currents of European art, might have led to a distinctively national style. But in the thirteenth century an influx of new ideas from France put an end to this particular line of development. The rise of the great Gothic cathedrals of France had dazzled Spanish churchmen, who now won the support of the kings for a church-building program of their own. Many Spanish churches (including those of Zamora, Santo Domingo de la Calzada, Ávila, Salamanca, Orense, Lérida, and Tarragona) had over the past few decades been built in the so-called transitional style. Those built from the thirteenth century onwards followed French models much more closely.

French influence was in fact so strong that some buildings in Spain, like the cathedral of León, are as purely Gothic as anything in France. Inside, the wall surfaces were broken up by large stained-glass windows, and the slender piers and pointed arches introduced a new note of elegance and refinement. The ground-plan at León copies that of Rheims cathedral, with reductions and slight alterations. Some of its sculptured doorways, in particular that of the Last Judgment in the center of the west front, are thought to be the work of French artists from Champagne. The naturalism implicit in Master Mateo's figures has here been given emphatic expression. The group of the elect, in the lower part of the Last Judgment tympanum, shows a profoundly humanized vision of eternal glory. Some of the figures are talking quietly together, while another plays the organ, helped by a man working the bellows. Among the elect are some Franciscans, who, as Sánchez Cantón has pointed out, played an important part in the history of art. Spanish sculpture was penetrated by a vitalizing current of warm, human feeling that reflected a profound change in men's sensibilities.

Two influential saints who are worthy of comparison with St Bernard must not be forgotten in the great century of Gothic art: St Francis of Assisi, founder of the Franciscan order, and a Spaniard, St Dominic of Guzman, founder of the Dominicans, both of whom gave new directions and a fresh sense of purpose to the religious life. The friar took the place of the monk, the order that of the monastery. Instead of seeking salvation in a flight from the world and from town life, the new religious orders proposed to act *in* the world, *in* the towns, and to remedy evil through direct, friendly contact with the people. St Dominic's preaching had its best result in combating serious disorders like that of the Albigensian heretics. St Francis of Assisi, working in a completely different spirit, gave rise to a more optimistic view of life and a closer feeling of communion between man and nature.

It is worth noting, however, that by the time the friars became active in the towns, the thirteenth century was already well advanced, whereas the new emphasis on reality in art, with subjects taken directly from nature, had already appeared in the second half of the previous century. For this reason it would seem that the changes in religious life were the result of fundamental changes taking place in the whole of the life around it.

The great Spanish cathedrals of the thirteenth century were those of Burgos and Toledo, which show again how strong was the influence of French art on the kingdom of Castile. In point of style, however, they already diverge from the pure Gothic of León cathedral. Gradually the first steps were being taken towards what might be called the "hispanization" of Gothic. In Burgos the plan is that of a Latin cross, which may possibly be explained by Cistercian influence, while the elevation is comparable to that of Bourges. But as a whole Burgos cathedral has a personality of its own that grew even more pronounced with the additions (west spires, chapel of the Constable, lantern over the transept) made in the fifteenth and sixteenth centuries.

LEÓN CATHEDRAL: STAINED-GLASS WINDOWS IN THE APSE. LATE 13TH AND EARLY 14TH CENTURY.

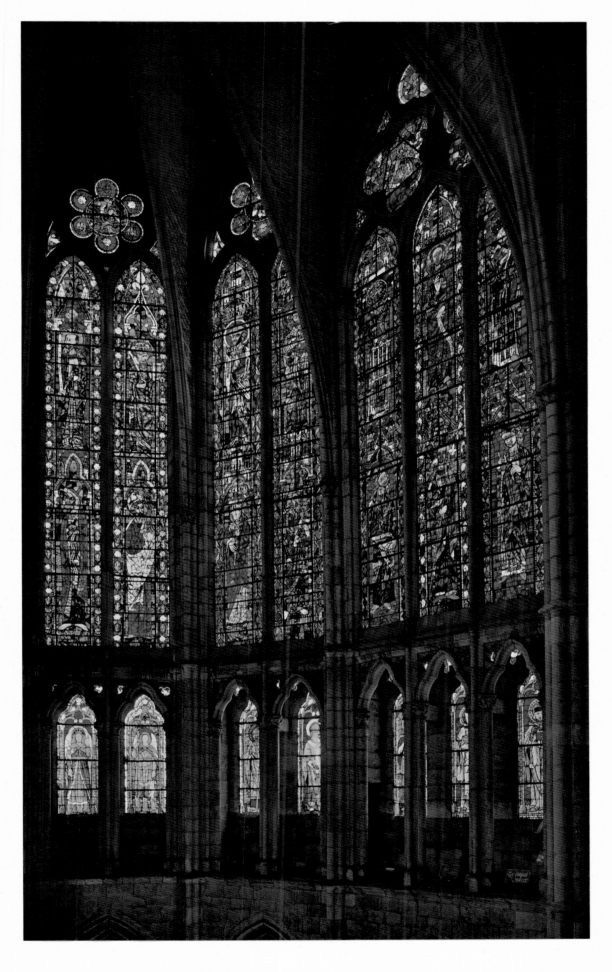

LEÓN CATHEDRAL: STAINED-GLASS WINDOWS IN THE APSE. LATE 13TH AND EARLY 14TH CENTURY.

Artists from Champagne evidently worked on the sculpture at Burgos. The finest group is in the doorway of the south transept, the Puerta del Sarmental, where a composition of Romanesque origin, Christ in Majesty surrounded by the symbols of the Evangelists, is given a new meaning: the figure of Jesus becomes more human, and the eagle of St John, the bull of St Luke, the lion of St Mark, and the angel of St Matthew are modelled with complete realism. Beside their four symbols, the Evangelists themselves sit writing at desks that faithfully copy those used at the time.

The cathedral of Toledo, with its five-aisled nave forming a vast hall, has been compared in its structure with Notre-Dame in Paris, and with Le Mans and Bourges, but none of these cathedrals is in fact its model. It is a church that is full of character, incorporating all kinds of ideas and techniques, but finally combining them into a coherent whole. The design of the ambulatory, with its alternately triangular and rectangular bays, was highly original compared with earlier ones. The transept does not project beyond the outer walls of the nave, whose spatial organization, by varying the height of the aisles, creates a sense of unity and amplitude.

The original building has suffered more than any other Spanish cathedral from a great many additions that have radically altered its appearance. Cloister, chapels, chapter house, sacristy, portals, choir, altars and tombs illustrate, almost step by step, the evolution of Spanish art from the thirteenth century until our own time. Few cathedrals in the world have treasures to rival those of Toledo cathedral, and for this reason, hemmed in as it is between narrow streets, it is a symbol of what each generation has left behind it.

The Gothic spirit appears at its best in the statue of the Virgin and Child in the choir. The Virgin is no longer the throne of God, as she was in Romanesque sculpture, but a mother holding her child; and her expression is full of tenderness as the child, smiling, caresses her chin. This polychrome figure is one of the most beautiful European statues of the thirteenth century, and was probably made by a French artist. So it is yet another sign of the strength of French influence in Spanish art.

Gothic art in Castile produced a rich variety of works. But after the brilliant period lasting throughout the whole of the thirteenth century, in which it so creatively assimilated French influence, a humdrum period followed, during the fourteenth century, in which forms seemed to be stagnant. But the last century of the Middle Ages, close to the time of the Catholic Kings, brought a revival of all the arts in Castile.

In the kingdom of Aragon, with Catalonia as its center, things were otherwise. From the Romanesque period on, architecture here had steadily gained in originality and importance. But, unlike Castile, Aragon did not reach its height architecturally in the second half of the twelfth or in the thirteenth century. Some important buildings of

THE VIRGIN AND CHILD. 13TH CENTURY. ALABASTER STATUE IN THE CHOIR OF TOLEDO CATHEDRAL.

that time exist, but it was not until the fourteenth century that the forms of Aragonese architecture achieved full maturity and character. The art of northeastern Spain was influenced mainly by southern France and Italy, as a result of active political and, above all, commercial relations between them. It quickly took on a personality of its own and, owing to the presence of Catalans in other Mediterranean countries, spread far beyond the borders of Catalonia. A great many Spanish elements appear in the art of Sicily, Sardinia and Cyprus, and even in that of the Greek mainland, where the kings of Aragon held the Duchy of Athens.

Catalan Gothic has its point of departure in the great Cistercian monasteries of Poblet and Santas Creus and in some of the cathedrals in the transitional style, like Lérida and Tarragona. It began very soberly and (which is surprising) this structural simplicity was maintained until the fifteenth century. Churches with large stained-glass windows and complicated flying buttresses are not characteristic of Catalonia, where window openings are reduced in number and the structure is very simple. Instead of the differences in height between the aisles of the nave, which give a broken outline to French churches, we generally find very spacious interiors. Many churches have a single undivided nave and even when there are three aisles there is little difference in height between them. Chapels open into the side walls between the buttresses, thus being incorporated in the very structure of the building.

The Cistercian spirit seems to have survived a long time in the churches of eastern Spain, checking the natural evolution of their forms. It is surprising, considering the importance of sculpture in other fields, how little they contain in the way of monumental sculpture. The portals of churches in Catalonia, Valencia and Majorca are nearly always distinguished by their sparing use of figure carvings and reliefs; and inside, the finest effects are achieved through the contrast between the bare walls and the altarpieces (painted or sculptured) and magnificent tombs.

A few highly representative churches show how religious architecture developed in eastern Catalonia. The cathedral of Barcelona, which has a three-aisled nave, a transept that does not project beyond the outer walls, an ambulatory, and chapels in the recesses between the buttresses, was begun in 1298. What is surprising about it is not only the size of its side aisles, which rise almost to the full height of the nave, but the spatial effects achieved by the open galleries over the chapels. The polygonal towers above the transept give character to the east end.

Santa María del Mar, in Barcelona, which was also built in the fourteenth century, is in some ways similar to the cathedral. It has three aisles and a series of chapels recessed between the buttresses; its spacious interior is particularly impressive. In its external design, it is the archetype of the churches of eastern Spain, with bare walls that seem to enclose cubic volumes. At each end of the main façade rises a small polygonal tower.

INTERIOR OF PALMA CATHEDRAL, MAJORCA. 14TH-16TH CENTURY.

COURTYARD OF THE PALACIO DE LA DIPUTACIÓN, BARCELONA. 15TH CENTURY.

The cathedral of Gerona is one of the most remarkable examples in the world of the bold use of space in the interior. Work was begun at the east end, the original plan providing for a three-aisled nave. But when the builders finished the aisled choir and reached the transept, it was decided to complete the cathedral with an aisleless nave equal in width to the choir and its side aisles. It was thus, at the beginning of the fifteenth century, when the original plan of Gerona cathedral was changed, that eastern Spanish Gothic took its obsession with vast spaces as far as it would go.

The cathedral of Valencia was unfortunately much altered in the eighteenth century, and its piers, arches and vaults were masked by a neoclassical covering. But the Gothic bell-tower of El Miguelete remains, which is taller than any other polygonal tower of its kind in eastern Spain.

The cathedral of Palma, in Majorca, has a very special place among the Gothic cathedrals of Aragon. It is not the latest in date, though it was built very slowly. Work on it may have started in the thirteenth century, but the main fabric was raised in the fourteenth and the early decades of the fifteenth; a few vaults were completed in the sixteenth. Both inside and outside it is impressive for its architectural massiveness.

A few measurements will give an idea of its proportions: the total length is 397 feet, the width 180; the height of the nave is 131 feet, that of the side aisles 98. These figures show enough of its volume to allow comparison with other churches in eastern Spain. The large number of buttresses, flying buttresses and pinnacles, on the other hand, suggest French churches. Palma cathedral has often been compared with the framework of an overturned wooden ship.

The interior produces an impression of great simplicity and spaciousness. Slender, unadorned octagonal piers (with iron lamps twined round them, designed by the famous modern architect Antonio Gaudí) divide the central nave from the side aisles, on to which open large chapels that further increase the size of the church. The nave is roofed with simple cross-vaults with none of the elaborate decoration of Late Gothic. The windows between the buttresses are very narrow; but the large rose-windows in the apse flood the whole interior with light. With all its contrasts, Palma cathedral brings the religious architecture of eastern Spain to a brilliant conclusion.

Aragon also has some notable examples of civil architecture in this period. They are of particular interest as indicating the relative importance of the Aragonese cities in the later Middle Ages. Here the situation contrasted strongly with that in Castile, where large mansions were not built until the time of the Catholic Kings. In Aragon, there were plenty from the fourteenth century onwards. There was another type of secular building, too, which did not exist in the other Christian kingdoms—this was the Lonja (commercial exchange), which artistically had closer links with Italy than with France.

CRUCIFIX CARVED IN JET. ABOUT 13TH CENTURY (WITH 15TH-CENTURY ADDITIONS). MUSEUM OF PONTEVEDRA, GALICIA.

Civil architecture in eastern Spain had the same simplicity of design as religious architecture, and this is found even in military constructions. Two eloquent examples are the Puerta de Serranos in Valencia, built by Pedro Balaguer at the end of the fourteenth century; and the castle of Bellver overlooking the city of Palma. In the first, its function as a defensive gateway in the old city walls is combined perfectly with graceful design and a sense of artistic fitness. Between two large polygonal towers the archway of the entrance is decorated with rich Gothic tracery, suggesting the presence—imaginary of course—of large open windows. The castle of Bellver in Majorca is a massive circular fortress with a central courtyard surrounded by arcades with pointed arches. This highly original form has no antecedent in Spanish art and practically no imitations, because it is by no means sure that Pedro Machuca had this circular courtyard in mind when he designed the palace of Charles V at Granada. A prominent feature of the castle of Bellver is a detached watch-tower of great size, joined to the main building by a bridge. This type of detached tower is characteristic of Islamic architecture, and its presence at Bellver can be explained only through some outside influence from the Mediterranean world.

The palaces of eastern Spain show a radical contrast with those of Castile. Their sober façades, for one thing, make them quite different. But much more noticeable are the differences in the plan of the courtyard. In the Palacio de la Diputación in Barcelona, for instance, the staircase in the courtyard is external, interrupting the series of arches that unfold on all four sides. Decoration is reduced to openwork disks on the staircase and the railings of the main floor, and the effect is extremely elegant, with very slender colonnettes supporting pointed arches. The construction of this palace was in progress in 1425 and, with all its Italian refinements, it is a very beautiful prototype.

The Lonjas, or commercial exchanges, illustrate another aspect of civil architecture in eastern Spain. They are designed on somewhat different lines in Aragon, Catalonia, Valencia, and the Balearic Islands, but all of them are characterized by a spacious interior with a vaulted roof on a single level. The Lonja at Palma, in Majorca, is one of the finest buildings in the island. Designed by Guillermo Sagrera, who also worked on Palma cathedral, it was built in the second quarter of the fifteenth century. Outwardly it looks like a small castle, whereas inside, the rib-vaults are supported by columns with deep, spiral flutings. These and other features give a touch of Orientalism to the spacious interior. This Lonja served as a model for the Silk Exchange in Valencia, built towards the end of the fifteenth century.

In this survey of Gothic architecture down to the time of the Catholic Kings, it only remains to note the important part played by sculpture and painting in the development of new forms. The new idea of spirituality appeared, as we have seen, in a series of monumental sculptures which initiated an art that was profoundly human, in which joy and sorrow were conveyed directly, without abstractions or symbols.

From the Portico de la Gloria in Santiago de Compostela to the free-standing figure of the Virgin and Child in the cathedral of Toledo, we can trace the progress of Gothic naturalism. But in addition to these works, with their strong personal imprint, there are others whose interest lies in the light they throw on the way in which forms evolved in the passage from Romanesque to Gothic. A signal example is the cross, carved in jet, in the museum of Pontevedra, in Galicia. Reproduced here for the first time, it combines stylistic elements of very different origins.

The discovery of the Pontevedra cross has greatly extended our knowledge of jet-carving. An extremely dense variety of lignite coal, jet is so shiny that it has been compared with black glass. Brittle and hard to work, it was known in ancient times, and used for artistic purposes during the Middle Ages in Galicia. Jet objects were commonly believed to be an effective charm against the evil eye and other superstitions, so they were prized as amulets and used as such in Spain from at least the eleventh century. The oldest surviving example is a tiny hand-shaped pendant worn about the neck, found in Granada among some thirteenth-century coins. The first workshops of jet-carvers in Santiago de Compostela, who turned out a great many objects and trinkets bought by the pilgrims, may have been set up about this time. Many of their carvings represent the apostle St James with the attributes of the pilgrims to his shrine at Santiago—staff, pouch, hat and cockleshells. Thus the talismanic properties of jet were combined with a devotional significance. Jet is so difficult to work that the relief generally suffers from a certain coarseness. The Pontevedra cross is a notable exception, the quality of the carving being unusually fine.

The dead Christ is represented hanging on the cross, in accordance with Gothic iconography; he is the Man of Sorrows, in contrast with the hieratic image of the living Christ in Romanesque art. Yet there are a number of elements in the Pontevedra cross which appear to derive directly from the Romanesque ivory crucifix of King Ferdinand and Queen Sancha (cf. pages 100-101). The manner in which hair and beard are rendered is quite similar, and there are points of similarity between the decoration of the jet cross and the themes and ornamental motifs of the ivory crucifix from León. By way of the latter, a certain Orientalism was thus transmitted to the jet cross. This unique carving can, in the main, be dated to the thirteenth century, although a few of the smaller reliefs on it, such as the one representing the Virgin and Child, may have been added towards the end of the fifteenth century.

Turning to another field of the minor arts, we find some splendid examples of Gothic miniature painting in a group of illuminated manuscripts of the *Cantigas* (songs in honor of the Virgin), written by King Alfonso X the Wise. The miniatures in the three *Cantigas* manuscripts preserved in the Escorial, the National Library in Madrid and the Laurentian Library in Florence represent the miracles of the Virgin in a sequence of scenes whose appeal stems not only from their charming naturalness, but above

PERE JOHAN (15TH CENTURY): ST GEORGE SLAYING THE DRAGON. 1418. RELIEF.
PALACIO DE LA DIPUTACIÓN, BARCELONA.

all from the easy and telling flow of the narrative. Life, in these scenes, is viewed directly, and the supernatural is discreetly fitted into the setting of everyday life. Guerrero Lovillo has shown the extent to which Oriental and Occidental elements are mingled and fused in these miniature paintings. The garments worn by the figures, the buildings, furniture, weapons and so on, all conjure up a lively and authentic picture of daily life in thirteenth-century Spain. While wholly in the spirit of Gothic art, the *Cantigas* miniatures are also profoundly Spanish: the Christian scenes are enacted against a background of Moorish motifs.

CANTIGAS (SONGS IN HONOR OF THE VIRGIN) OF ALFONSO X THE WISE: MINIATURE ILLUSTRATING SONG LII. 13TH CENTURY.
MONASTERY OF THE ESCORIAL, NEAR MADRID.

From the fourteenth century onwards, the Gothic art of Spain, both in sculpture and painting, is represented by a whole series of masters and schools who, in the various Christian kingdoms, gave variety and individuality to the new style.

The high tide of Gothic painting and sculpture in Spain covers the period from about 1300 to 1450. During this time more and more emphasis was given to narrative scenes, both in the reliefs on sculptured tombs and in carved or painted altarpieces. It was in Aragon that this artistic activity flourished most, although work of high quality was being done in all the kingdoms. The economic well-being which a maritime district enjoys (for Catalonia, as we have noted, had been united to the kingdom of Aragon) must have contributed a great deal to this surge of activity.

FERRER BASSA (ACTIVE 1324-1348): THE NATIVITY. 1345-1346. WALL PAINTING IN OILS. CONVENT OF PEDRALBES (BARCELONA).

The most brilliant phase of Catalan sculpture began at the end of the thirteenth century with Master Bartolomeu, who was active in Tarragona. The royal tombs in the monastery of Santas Creus, near Tarragona, dating to the first third of the fourteenth century, seem to reflect a combination of Italian and French influences, easily explained by the political conditions of the time. The influence of Pisan sculpture—the school, that is, of Nicola and Giovanni Pisano—is found in works like the tomb of St Eulalia, patroness of the city, in Barcelona cathedral. In the second half of the fourteenth century, several outstanding artists, such as Aloy and Jaime Cascalls, came to the fore in Catalonia. It was Aloy Cascalls who carved the retable in the Capilla de los Sastres (i.e. the Tailors' Chapel) in the cathedral of Tarragona.

Jaime Cascalls, who collaborated with Aloy in some tombs in the monastery of Poblet, also had a share in several retables. His pupil and assistant was a Greek slave who had two sons and taught them both the art of sculpture. The younger, Pere Johan, who worked in the first half of the fifteenth century, is undoubtedly the most gifted sculptor Catalonia produced during the Middle Ages. The main altarpiece in the cathedral of Tarragona, which he carved in alabaster, shows a great step forward from the retable in the Capilla de los Sastres: not only is the decoration richer, but the reliefs are skillfully laid out on several planes seen in perspective, so as to create a pictorial effect, just as in the work of Pere Johan's great Florentine contemporary Ghiberti.

Pere Johan's most successful work is the relief of St George on horseback that decorates the front of the Palacio de la Diputación in Barcelona. The artist inscribed a circle in a square, and within it set the figure of the saint, with the dragon at his feet. The carving of the framework shows his fine sense of decorative effect: in the spandrels he placed thistles, flowers, tracery, and in each corner a head. The dragon is lying on its back, and although its head is mortally wounded, the convulsive movement of its body still betrays the tension of the fight. The horse, with its legs splayed out, conveys an impression of movement through the saddlecloth that streams over its hind quarters as if whipped by the wind. St George, in armor and holding a shield, is thrusting his lance (which has disappeared) into the dragon's head; halter, trappings and shield all have delicate decorations on them. This fine piece of stone carving must have been made shortly after the construction of the Palacio began in 1416.

Outside Catalonia, Gothic sculpture up to about the middle of the fifteenth century found its finest expression in the kingdom of Navarre, where French influences were paramount. It was two French masters who introduced the Burgundian style into Spain through their works in the cathedral of Pamplona: Jacques Perut, with his Adoration of the Kings in the cloister, and Janin Lomme, with his tombs of Charles III the Noble and his queen, Leonor of Castile. In the latter, the recumbent figures of Charles and Leonor, and above all the figures of the hooded friars grouped around the tomb, are the first indications of the influence of Claus Sluter in Spain, about 1420.

RAMÓN DE MUR (?-AFTER 1435): THE NATIVITY. 1402-1412. PANEL OF THE GUIMERÁ ALTARPIECE. EPISCOPAL MUSEUM, VICH (BARCELONA).

ANONYMOUS MASTER: ALTARPIECE OF FRAY BONIFACIO FERRER. ABOUT 1400. SAN CARLOS MUSEUM, VALENCIA.

The altarpiece of the Holy Spirit in the collegiate church of Manresa, painted in 1394, is Pedro Serra's most representative work and one that well reflects the influence of Italian Trecento painting. This well-organized Gothic altarpiece comprises a complex series of panels arranged in vertical and horizontal rows, divided vertically by narrow strips decorated with full-length figures of saints. The imagery presents a certain novelty in the scenes from the New Testament and the Old (notably the panels with Adam and the Creation of the World) and in the scenes from saints' lives at each end of the predella. The oblong panel in the center of the predella, a Pietà by Luis Borrassá, painted in 1411, was subsequently added to Serra's altarpiece.

Painted half a century later, the altarpiece of the Transfiguration in Barcelona cathedral, by Bernardo Martorell, reflects the changes brought about in the interval under the stimulus of foreign influences. The love of details for their own sake, so characteristic of the International Style that had now superseded Italian Gothic, appears here with other distinctive traits of this delicate master. The three predella panels and the six larger scenes above them illustrate themes especially chosen to exalt Christ's divinity, such as the Transfiguration and various miracles. The rendering of the Crucifixion and the Descent from the Cross is full of dramatic feeling.

The altarpiece of Fray Bonifacio Ferrer is roughly contemporary with Pedro Serra's altarpiece. It exemplifies the transition from Italian Gothic art to the International Style at Valencia, an art center in some ways quite distinct from Catalonia. The transitional character of its style accounts for the fact that it has been attributed to several masters, though to none convincingly. In any case it is the work of an artist with a personality of his own, a contemporary of Pedro Nicolau, Lorenzo Zaragoza and Marçal de Sax.

The position of Spanish art in relation to that of other European countries during the Gothic period is seen most clearly in the field of painting. After the ferment of the Romanesque period, Spain became receptive to a number of outside influences, though even under their impact each kingdom retained its own distinctive mode of expression. Roughly speaking, and allowing for exceptions, it may be said—keeping to the traditional terms of classification—that French influence was dominant in the thirteenth century, and Italian in the fourteenth; the International Style, so called because of its hybrid character, triumphed in the first half of the fifteenth century, while in the second half Flemish influence prevailed.

The Franco-Gothic or linear style of painting made its appearance in the later altar frontals and found its maturest expression, at the end of the thirteenth and the beginning of the fourteenth century, in wall paintings whose area of diffusion extended all over northern Spain, from Catalonia to Castile. Elements deriving from French art are often found side by side with details of Moorish origin.

Italian Gothic influences were so strong and persistent that they led to a rapid assimilation of the art of Florence and Siena. These influences made their greatest impact in Catalonia, which had close commercial ties with Italy and was in contact with the papal court at Avignon as well, where Italian artists were patronized and works of art brought in from Italy. The Sienese style is best reflected in the work of Ferrer Bassa, who was active between 1324 and 1348. His masterpiece is the series of wall paintings in the chapel of St Michael in the convent of the Poor Clares at Pedralbes, near Barcelona. Scenes from the Annunciation to the Crucifixion are arranged in two groups (the Life of the Virgin and the Passion); all reflect unmistakably the influence of Italian Trecento painting, in particular that of Simone Martini, who had worked at Avignon.

Wholly in the spirit and style of Simone is the composition of the Virgin and Child surrounded by angels, and certain mannerisms, such as that of lengthening the eyes, are typical of the Sienese master. Some of the scenes, such as the Arrest of Christ, with St Peter cutting off the ear of Malchus, have an expressive power worthy of Giotto.

It is clear from all this that the new ideas that had transformed painting in Italy were developed very early in Spain. Catalonia experienced them sooner than other parts of Spain, and there, within the space of a few years, artists and ateliers appeared that proceeded to diffuse the Italian Gothic style. After Ferrer Bassa, the most gifted master was probably Pedro Serra, member of a family of painters (including his brother Jaime) who were active in Catalonia during the last third of the fourteenth century. Pedro Serra's art is finely represented in the altarpiece of the Holy Spirit in the church of Santa María at Manresa. This work is an important landmark in the evolution of the painted altarpiece, which followed a line of development roughly parallel to that of the sculptured altarpiece.

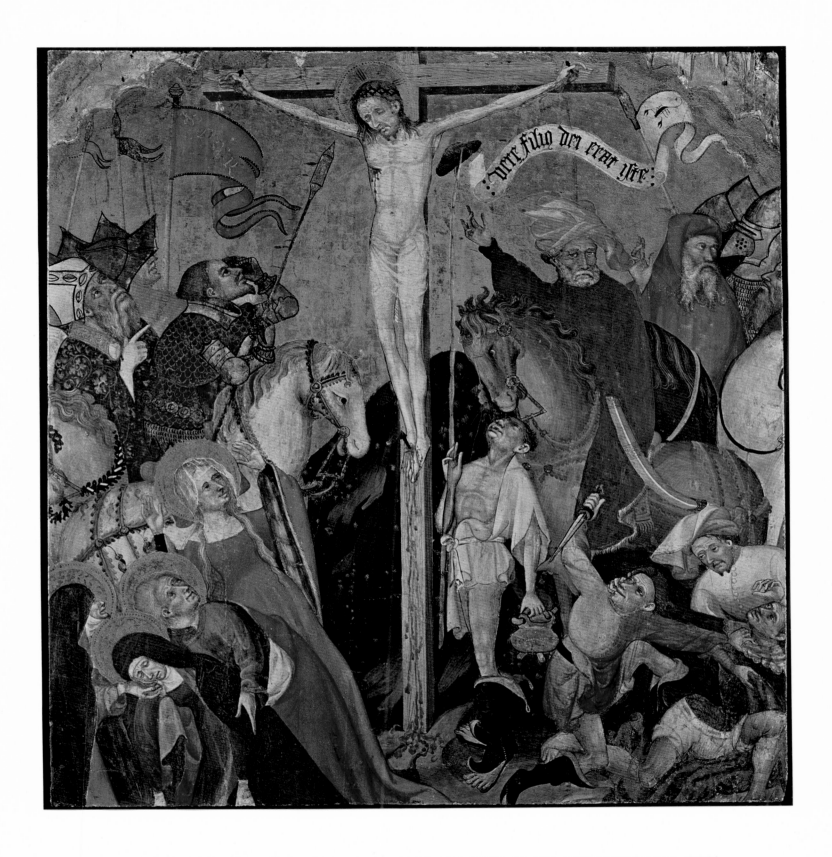

LUIS BORRASSÁ (ACTIVE 1380-1424): THE CRUCIFIXION. 1411. PANEL OF THE ALTARPIECE OF SAN PEDRO.
CHURCH OF SANTA MARÍA, TARRASA.

The Manresa altarpiece consists of five series of vertical panels divided by six narrow vertical strips, standing on a base or predella to which several painted panels were added later. The large central panel depicts Pentecost or the Descent of the Holy Spirit: the figure of the Virgin, seated among the assembled Apostles, "all filled with the Holy Ghost" (Acts ii), is more relaxed and realistic than Ferrer Bassa's Virgins. In many other panels that take us from the Creation to scenes from the Gospels, Pedro Serra arranges figure groups very ably and adds landscape backgrounds with an intuitive feeling for perspective. Painted in 1394, the Manresa altarpiece sums up the Tuscan influences acting on Catalan painting during the fourteenth century.

There sprang up in the entourage of the Serra brothers a whole group of masters, whose work is gradually being sorted out and identified; with them the influence of Italian Gothic painting reached its height throughout eastern Spain. But from about 1400 on the new trends that produced the International Style rapidly gained ground.

The common features of this style, characteristic of many artists all over Europe, were a preoccupation with anecdote, a spiritualizing of forms, a mannered elegance and elongated proportions in the figures. One of the outstanding masters of the International Style was Luis Borrassá, who produced a large number of paintings during the first quarter of the fifteenth century. He was a native of Gerona, in northern Catalonia, where he must have been trained and where he may have known some French painters. He then moved to Barcelona, where his style came to maturity in contact with other masters. His development can be traced through a number of surviving altarpieces, one of the most expressive being that of the church of San Pedro at Tarrasa, now preserved in the local museum of Santa María. It seems to have been dedicated to St Peter. In some scenes, such as the one of St Peter walking on the water, with fishermen plying their nets in the immediate background and Jesus helping the Apostle out of the Lake of Tiberias, he manages to focus attention on the main subject, while giving almost equal prominence to details which are purely anecdotal. The Crucifixion, which crowns the altarpiece, is very characteristic. The elongated body of Christ shows Borrassá to be a true representative of the International Style.

One of his contemporaries was Ramón de Mur, whose finest work is the Guimerá altarpiece in the museum of Vich. Records of the period show that he spent ten years working on it, from 1402 to 1412. Each of its various panels is painted with careful attention to the smallest detail, and every theme serves as a pretext for anecdotal elements handled with the utmost ingenuity. In the vision of Paradise this is particularly so: plants, birds, deer, and exotic animals are rendered with remarkable imagination. In the scene of the Nativity, the child Jesus tightly wrapped in swaddling clothes lies in a disproportionately large crib or manger, ornately carved in wood. The wealth of details is such that the eye, drawn away from the main theme, strays curiously from one to another: the ornamental carving of the manger, the nailed planks forming the stable roof, the conventional rocks suggesting a landscape, the tiny figures of the shepherds leaning on their staff as they look up at the Angel of the Annunciation.

The International Style in Catalonia came to a brilliant close with Bernardo Martorell, a painter of very great gifts who, until his identity was revealed by a study of contemporary records, was called the Master of St George after his most famous work: the altarpiece divided between the Art Institute of Chicago (which owns the central panel with St George slaying the dragon) and the Louvre. The discovery of his name in 1937, and the attribution to him of a series of works, meant that his activity could be documented in the second quarter of the fifteenth century. The outstanding characteristic of Martorell's style is poise and elegance. No other Spanish Gothic painter seems to have reached a comparable degree of refinement. His drawing is always very delicate and meticulous, and the anecdotal elements, numerous though they are, never detract from the main theme. His strength, in fact, probably lies in this perfect harmony between the essential and the accessory.

In 1449 Bernardo Martorell painted the altarpiece of the Transfiguration in the cathedral of Barcelona. The central scene, of the transfigured Christ surrounded by the Apostles, has all the dignity the subject demands. Some panels, such as the one showing the Descent from the Cross, are deeply emotive, but probably the most famous is that of the Marriage at Cana. The large earthenware jars give a distinctive character to the whole scene; the tall, slender figures have a kind of stately animation, and the objects on the table are rendered with detailed realism.

Martorell brings to a close one cycle of Catalan painting; Luis Dalmau opens another in 1445. This was the period of Flemish influence, and the Virgin of the Councillors is the first Spanish painting that shows the impact of Jan van Eyck. It appears from documents that Dalmau, who came from Valencia, was sent to Flanders by Alfonso V of Aragon, and so very likely had direct contact with Van Eyck; indeed, he may have been present when Van Eyck's great polyptych of the Adoration of the Lamb was installed in the church of St Bavo at Ghent in 1432. Certainly Dalmau's own altarpiece of the Virgin of the Councillors, which he signed in 1445, is the work of a man who has carefully studied and assimilated Van Eyck's style.

The Virgin of the Councillors has further importance, for it strongly influenced Catalan painters in the second half of the fifteenth century. In the middle of the painting is a large Gothic throne, on which Mary sits with the Child on her lap, the latter draped in a transparent veil. On either side, kneeling in an attitude of prayer, are the city fathers (or councillors) of Barcelona commended by their patron saints Andrew and Eulalia. In the background are open windows thronged with singing figures, as in Van Eyck's Ghent altarpiece. Beyond them, on the horizon, are distant plains and the minutely detailed shapes of conventional buildings that so often appear in Flemish

LUIS DALMAU (ACTIVE 1428-1460): THE VIRGIN OF THE COUNCILLORS. 1445. MUSEUM OF CATALAN ART, BARCELONA.

paintings. In addition to the elements taken from the Ghent altarpiece, the figure of Dalmau's Virgin closely resembles the Virgin prayed to by Canon Van der Paele in Van Eyck's famous painting in Bruges.

The part played by Dalmau in introducing the Flemish style into Catalonia gives him a place beside his contemporary Martorell. But the paintings produced at Valencia in the International Style during the first half of the fifteenth century were quite worthy of comparison with those of Catalonia. The altarpiece of Fray Bonifacio Ferrer, which was given to the Carthusian monastery of Portaceli and today is in the San Carlos Museum in Valencia, must have been painted about 1400. Above a predella with five small scenes on it are three large vertical panels showing the Crucifixion (in the center) between the Conversion of St Paul and the Baptism of Christ. Crowning the three is the Last Judgment, with the figures of the Annunciation on either side. The contrast in size between the various scenes underlines the monumentality of the three main panels.

The unknown master who painted this altarpiece took great care to distinguish each subject by giving it special features, and conceiving the figures in a very distinct way. But he could not or would not give up the anecdotes, which distract the spectator. Thus, around the Crucifixion, he grouped seven small scenes showing the sacraments.

Around 1400 Pedro Nicolau was also working in Valencia; but although he was contemporary with the Master of the Bonifacio Ferrer Altarpiece, his qualities were very different. What is most attractive about Nicolau is the tenderness that appears especially in works showing the Virgin and Child, such as the Sarrión altarpiece, which recalls Sienese paintings of the same kind (among them Simone Martini's *Maestà*, for instance), though Nicolau's figures are more slender and graceful, are set further apart, and even have a certain melancholy air about them.

The International Style spread to other parts of Spain as well. With many Italian echoes, it appears in the work of the master who painted the panels of the reliquary triptych from the monastery of Piedra, in Aragon. Other artists in Aragon and Navarre had a more forceful and vigorous way of expressing themselves. Castile was influenced by Italian Gothic through the presence there of Italian painters like Gherardo Starnina, to whom works in Toledo have been attributed, and above all Nicolás Florentino, who painted the main altarpiece in the old cathedral of Salamanca in the middle of the fifteenth century. Despite the activity of these Italian Gothic masters, the International Style developed uninterruptedly during the first half of the fifteenth century, and we find it well characterized in the work of Nicolás Francés. Spanish Gothic painting had a complex history between the thirteenth and the mid-fifteenth centuries, and it cannot be examined in any detail here; but Spanish artists were all this time in fruitful contact with the art of other countries, and their work benefited from an influx of European art trends.

PAINTING ON SHEEPSKIN. 15TH CENTURY. CEILING OF THE HALL OF THE KINGS, ALHAMBRA, GRANADA.

A decisive proof of the importance and influence of Spain's integration in Europe appears in the last of the Moorish kingdoms: in the Alhambra at Granada. In the vaulting of the Hall of the Kings, beside the Court of the Lions, there are three curious scenes painted on sheepskin. The painting in the central vault represents an assembly of kings, while the other two, on either side of it, show scenes of a knightly character with Christians, Moors, fair ladies, animals and hairy savages. The subject matter of these paintings is extremely puzzling. One of them, reproduced here, appears to depict some legend of knights and ladies. But the European atmosphere that pervades the two side pictures is in marked contrast with the Oriental tone of the central scene.

Were these paintings the work of Christian artists summoned to the Moorish court of Granada? Or were they by a local artist who was familiar with Western painting? The first seems the more plausible explanation. Although natural scenery is painted in the background with a minuteness reminiscent of Persian miniatures, and although there are many details that in Christian countries would seem exotic, the dominant themes, the types of buildings and the character of the anecdotes suggest the forms that occasionally triumph in European miniatures and tapestries of the Late Gothic period. The paintings in the Alhambra must have been done at about that time, when a new age in Spanish art was about to begin, opening out on wider horizons.

THE APPROACH OF THE RENAISSANCE

The last stage of Spain's integration in the main currents of European art took place in one of the most critical periods of Spanish history—the period between the date generally accepted as the starting point of the modern age in the West, 1453 (the fall of Constantinople to the Turks), and the date which marks the beginning of the modern age in Spanish history, 1492 (the conquest of Granada from the Moors). During the second half of the fifteenth century the culture of the Italian Renaissance penetrated into several European countries, notably France and Spain. But in Spain the great transformation of art was not brought about by the leavening influence of Italy alone. The Spanish Renaissance owed much to the great renewal of the arts that had taken place in northern Europe, from Burgundy to Flanders.

The ferment of new ideas in Europe led to a fundamental revision of values in the second half of the fifteenth century, and the workings of this process were felt intensely in Spain. But the pressure of other tendencies, from the Moslem world, acted on the country as well, drawing it eastward again. For half a century Spanish life was subjected to acute tensions. To the grave political questions agitating Spain from within, were added many other problems abroad. Her progressive expansion in Italy (for the king of Aragon, Alfonso V, was also king of Naples) and the unexpected expansion of Spanish territory—America was discovered in the year that national unity was achieved, with the conquest of Granada—had profound effects on the whole of Spanish cultural life.

Two momentous events were the incorporation of the Moors of Granada into the Christian religion, and the expulsion of the Jews who refused to deny their faith. Economically, relations with Flanders, to which Spain exported raw materials, mainly wool, were very important. Thus in the space of a few years a country which throughout the Middle Ages had been concerned with purely internal problems was called on to play a leading part in European life, in preparation for the dominant position it was to occupy in the sixteenth century as a major power with an overseas empire.

The cultural changes of the fifteenth century took place against a background of stirring political events. In the middle of the century Spain was divided into four separate kingdoms. The kingdom of Castile was the largest, since it extended as far as the Atlantic seaboard, from the Basque country to Galicia, and covered the whole of the Castilian plateau and western Andalusia, from the valley of the Guadalquivir to the Portuguese frontier. The kingdom of Aragon included the region of Aragon proper, as well as Catalonia, Valencia, and the Balearic Islands. The kingdom of Navarre, as already noted, was hemmed in between Castile, Aragon and the Pyrenees, with no possibility of expansion. Finally, there survived at Granada, despite the stress of great internal crises, the last of the Moorish kingdoms, which dominated the Mediterranean coast from Almería to Málaga.

After the great conquests made in the thirteenth century by Ferdinand III the Holy, which culminated in the incorporation of Cordova and Seville, the kingdom of Castile was rent by internal struggles that did not really end until the time of Queen Isabella. Fratricidal wars to gain power, rivalries to hold it in the name of monarchs who were under age, public scandals caused by great nobles, court favor that degenerated into corruption—the history of nearly two centuries was made up of this, and more.

In 1454 King John II died. He was an unsuccessful ruler, but he surrounded himself with a cultivated court of poets like the Marquis de Santillana and Juan de Mena, both of whom watched with interest and admired all that was new from Italy. Santillana wrote sonnets "in the Italian style" and Juan de Mena's poetry was filled with humanistic feeling. King John's children were his successor on the throne of Castile, Henry IV (1454-1474), and Isabella the Catholic. In his day King Henry was known as "the Impotent," yet he acknowledged as his child, with a right to the throne, the daughter his second wife bore to her lover Don Beltrán de la Cueva. At Henry's death, Juana, called "la Beltraneja" by the people, claimed the crown, but after a civil war Isabella established herself as queen of Castile.

In Aragon, too, there was no lack of conflicts, from the time of James I (1213-1276), the contemporary of Ferdinand the Holy and conqueror of Valencia and Majorca, down to the reign of Ferdinand the Catholic (1479-1516). James's son, Peter III, captured Sicily in 1282, thus initiating that policy of expansion in the Mediterranean, above all in Italy, which was continued by his descendants. At the beginning of the fourteenth century Catalan troops were campaigning as far afield as Constantinople, and later they occupied Athens. Sardinia was fought for and acquired, and in the reign of Alfonso V (1416-1458) Naples was annexed to the crown of Aragon. Alfonso spent many years in Italy and when he died he divided his possessions, leaving his brother John II (1458-1479) those in the Iberian peninsula, together with Sardinia and Sicily. This namesake of the Castilian king was the father of Ferdinand the Catholic.

These historical circumstances in Castile and Aragon, the principal kingdoms of Spain at the end of the Middle Ages, must be borne in mind when we consider the happy fact of the marriage, in 1469, of Ferdinand and Isabella. For either to reign at all, some very unexpected things had had to happen. When they were born in the middle of the fifteenth century (Ferdinand in 1452, Isabella in 1451) no one could have foreseen that they would come to their respective thrones and finally achieve national unity. The death of Henry IV of Castile in 1474 and that of John II of Aragon in 1479 made it possible for the idea of unity to become a reality.

The two kingdoms of Castile and Aragon were ruled in common by Ferdinand and Isabella, and the new age began under the best auspices. With the conquest of Granada (1492) and, after Isabella's death (1504), the annexation of Navarre (1512), national unity was achieved; all efforts at union with Portugal had come to nothing. With religious unity achieved as well, and the power of the nobles checked, political expansion went ahead in America, and Spain was able to intervene actively in Italy as well.

Spanish art in this period is exceptionally rich and interesting, thanks to a concourse of artists of outstanding ability and very varied temperament. Foreign architects, sculptors and painters were attracted to Spain in great numbers, at a rate never to be seen again, and many of them settled there for good, becoming thoroughly hispanicized. At the same time a converse movement took place, as Spanish artists went to France, Flanders or Italy to complete their training: they played an important part in establishing contacts abroad and giving Spanish art the benefit of fresh stimuli. The result of this give-and-take was highly successful. By the beginning of the sixteenth century a certain maturity had been achieved, and the stage was set for the full development of Renaissance art in Spain.

The first current that influenced Spanish art in the fifteenth century came from Flanders. Trade relations between the two countries had led by now to an active interchange of raw materials, mainly wool, and manufactured products. One of the most valued articles in this growing volume of trade were works of art. In the fairs and bazaars of Spanish towns like Medina del Campo, in Castile, Flemish panel paintings were sold, and much sought after, for the realism of northern art appealed to Spaniards. How much these paintings were appreciated can be seen from the fine collection of them formed by Queen Isabella. The pictures listed in the original inventories (studied and published by F. J. Sánchez Cantón) were added to later, but only part of the collection has come down to us intact, preserved mainly in the Royal Chapel, Granada, and the Royal Palace, Madrid. Queen Isabella was especially fond of pictures on religious themes by Van der Weyden, Memlinc, Bosch and the masters she herself patronized, like Juan de Flandes and Michel Sithium.

Mention has already been made of Janin Lomme, the French sculptor who about 1420 made the tombs of King Charles III the Noble and Queen Leonor of Navarre, under the influence of Claus Sluter. This work stands out as the point of departure of much that was to come later. In 1427 the greatest Flemish painter of the day, Jan van Eyck, passed through Spain on his way to Portugal in the train of an ambassador; though we have no means of knowing what the immediate results of this journey may have been, it seems likely that it helped to arouse interest in his work in Spain. Contacts with Flanders were also strengthened by the Flemish pilgrims who came to Santiago de Compostela when the fame of the shrine of St James was revived during the fifteenth century.

GIL DE SILOE (ACTIVE 1486-1499): MAIN ALTARPIECE IN THE CARTHUSIAN MONASTERY OF MIRAFLORES (BURGOS). 1496-1499. WOOD.

The altarpiece of the Carthusian monastery of Miraflores (1496-1499), near Burgos, was carved by Gil de Siloe, who based the composition on a series of circles. Above a predella divided into two parts he set a great wheel, with four circles around it containing reliefs of the Evangelists writing the Gospels, and four more inside it showing scenes from the Passion. The central figure of Christ crucified, flanked by the Virgin and St John, stands out against this intricate composition. With its Gospel scenes, its figures of saints, its coats of arms, its fine carving and the coloring by Diego de la Cruz, this altarpiece is unique in its richness and originality. At the foot of the wheel is a turning device that allows the scenes to be changed according to the feasts of the year.

The altarpiece of Toledo cathedral (1498-1504) is bewilderingly rich: the entire work is covered with gold. Above the predella rise five vertical rows of reliefs, divided unevenly at various levels. In the scenes it is not so much the sculptural quality that counts as the richness of detail and decoration. The lowest level of the central row displays the great monstrance of gilt silver kept in the cathedral treasury. The altarpiece was designed by the French master Peti Juan, but other artists collaborated with him in its execution, among them Felipe de Borgoña, Copín de Holanda and Sebastián de Almonacid.

The altarpiece of Saragossa cathedral has a lower section carved by Pere Johan in the second quarter of the fifteenth century. Between 1470 and 1480 it was finished by Juan de Suabia (John of Swabia), who worked on the three scenes of the Transfiguration, the Adoration of the Magi, and the Ascension. The monstrance, the vessel in which the Eucharist was shown to the people, was placed in the center; this practice was retained in many Renaissance altarpieces in Aragon.

It was in the middle years of the fifteenth century that the great influx of northern artists into Spain took place. The first outstanding name is that of Hanequín de Bruselas (i.e. of Brussels), who was the master-artist at Toledo cathedral as early as 1448, and brought many collaborators, among them several members of his family. He was the moving spirit of Flamboyant Gothic art in Castile. His major work was the chapel containing the tomb of the constable Don Álvaro de Luna, prime minister of King John II; it is very richly decorated, and ogee arches, cusping, and thistle motifs are arranged in its fine tracery with an aesthetic sense akin to that of the Mudejar decorations in Toledo; indeed, the triumph of Flamboyant Gothic was facilitated by its close connection with works steeped in Orientalism.

In other parts of Toledo cathedral, too, the work of Hanequín de Bruselas confirms the triumph of the new style. Among these are the Puerta de los Leones (Portal of the Lions) which, in spite of alterations made in the eighteenth century that have impaired its stylistic unity, is still the handsomest of the cathedral doors. He had two assistants, Juan Alemán and Egas Cueman, and their teamwork seems to have been perfect. The sculptures on the doorposts and the archivolts, like the large carving in high relief showing the Tree of Jesse, are handled with vigorous naturalism. Thereafter northern artists became more numerous in Toledo and in the rest of Castile. One of the most representative was Juan Guas, who came from Brittany.

One of the most characteristic works of Juan Guas is the church and cloister of San Juan de los Reyes in Toledo. It was built to the order of Queen Isabella to celebrate the victory of Toro (1476), which was decisive in her struggle for the throne. The project had apparently been a very ambitious one and it seems that when the work began the queen was disappointed at the size of the church, which was not as large as she had hoped. Even so, San Juan de los Reyes is today one of the most attractive examples of Flamboyant Gothic in Spain and, better than any other, displays the distinctive features of the so-called Isabelline style of Flamboyant architecture in the late fifteenth century. As it so happened, the construction of the church covered the very years of Isabella's reign, from 1477 to 1504.

The polychrome statue of Isabella the Catholic praying, at the foot of the main altarpiece in the Royal Chapel of Granada, brings the series of the queen's portraits to a brilliant close. The earliest and most lifelike pictures of her were painted on panels. This one, a wood carving made long after her death, was probably the work of the great sculptor and architect from Burgos, Diego de Siloe, who came to Granada in 1528. Thirty years before, his father, Gil de Siloe, had represented the queen in the same attitude in the altarpiece of the Carthusian monastery of Miraflores. Between the two portraits lay a fertile period for Spanish art, one which takes us from Late Gothic to the full Renaissance. While working on this figure, Diego de Siloe had to depend for his inspiration on portraits made of Isabella when she was about forty years old. Its serene composition and its decoration reveal Siloe's Italian background, but the polychromy is characteristically Spanish.

DIEGO DE SILOE (ABOUT 1495-1563): QUEEN ISABELLA AT PRAYER. ABOUT 1535. POLYCHROME WOOD. ROYAL CHAPEL, GRANADA.

In its ground-plan and layout, San Juan de los Reyes at Toledo represents the type of church that finally became most characteristic of the period. It has an aisleless nave with side chapels in the recesses between the buttresses, a transept of the same width as the nave with its side chapels, a polygonal apse, and a choir located at the west end of the church. The two-storied cloister is built against the south side of the church. The decoration of the interior is extremely rich, revealing a complete and perfect fusion of Flamboyant Gothic and Mudejar. Some vaults are supported by ribs that, in the Moorish fashion, do not cross in the center, and stucco ornaments in the form of stalactites—a typically Moorish type of ornament—are used in the transept. The inscription that runs along the inside of the church has the same decorative purpose as Arabic inscriptions, although its lettering is Gothic. And even the systematic repetition of the arms of the Catholic Kings serves an aesthetic purpose that is purely Oriental. Thus Flamboyant Gothic was taken over and restyled in a distinctively Spanish way.

A particularly fine example of the secular architecture of this period is the Infantado Palace at Guadalajara, also designed by Juan Guas. Unfortunately it was badly damaged in a bombardment during the Spanish Civil War of 1936-1939. Most regrettable of all was the damage inflicted on the decorative sculpture which was perhaps the most prominent feature of the building. On the façade, in the courtyard, and in the Salón de los Linajes, the Flamboyant Gothic and Mudejar styles of decoration are again harmoniously combined. But side by side with these, there are timid signs of Italianism as well, in such things as the diamond-pointed studs that decorate the façade and recall the famous Schifanoia Palace at Ferrara. Thus did Spanish art broaden its outlook, and it is no accident that the Infantado Palace was built for the Mendoza family, which so actively promoted the introduction of the Renaissance into Spain.

Also in the service of the Catholic Kings was Enrique Egas, who was active in Spain from the last decade of the fifteenth century until his death in 1534. He was a master of all the stylistic resources of Flamboyant Gothic, to which he clung, never adjusting himself to the new style of Renaissance art, paradoxically called "antique," that was coming in from Italy. A nephew of Hanequín de Bruselas, Egas maintained the Flemish traditions in which he had been schooled. As master-artist of Toledo cathedral, he left some small works that do not allow us to judge his talent. He appears to have played a decisive part in the building of three hospitals planned while the Catholic Kings were still living: those of Santiago de Compostela, Toledo and Granada. All three have central courtyards surrounded by the sick-rooms. At Compostela it was originally intended to build a chapel with a courtyard on either side, while in the other two the plan was that of a cross, with arms approximately the same length, and with four courtyards around the cross. It was only in Granada that the complete plan was adopted, although the building itself was not finished until after the sixteenth century.

RODRIGO ALEMÁN (15TH CENTURY): SCENE OF THE CONQUEST OF GRANADA. 1489-1494. WOOD CARVING ON THE CHOIR STALL. TOLEDO CATHEDRAL.

The hospitals designed by Egas, though they contain Gothic elements, were overlaid with Renaissance additions, and they show the extent to which the reign of the Catholic Kings was a period of transition from the Middle Ages to modern times. These large buildings may in part have suggested the design adopted for the monastery of the Escorial in the last third of the sixteenth century. The construction of such hospitals is indicative of the vast program of social and political reform undertaken by the Catholic Kings.

A number of sculptors from the north—Flemings, Burgundians, Germans and others—also worked in Toledo and left their impress on the art of Castile, where they diffused a style of sculpture deriving from Claus Sluter. Some, as we have seen, collaborated on monumental sculptures like the Puerta de los Leones of Toledo cathedral. Others carved altarpieces, choir stalls and tombs.

TOMB OF DON MARTÍN VÁZQUEZ DE ARCE. 1486-1504. CHAPEL OF SANTA CATALINA, CATHEDRAL OF SIGÜENZA (GUADALAJARA).

In the time of the Catholic Kings, the art of wood carving produced some works of surpassing beauty in the choir stalls which, in line with a tradition that went back to the twelfth century at least, stood in the main nave of the churches. Magnificent reliefs went to decorate the panels on the backs and top part of the stalls, and also the elbow-rests or misericords (placed under the seats to allow the canons to rest against them while they stood praying). The wood, generally walnut, is not colored, and so had to be very carefully worked because no painting could be added afterwards to conceal flaws and corrections. Although they interrupt the view of the high altar, from the entrance of the church, these elaborately carved choir stalls are not only one of the most original features of the large Spanish churches, but also help materially to create an impression of greater spaciousness in the nave than is in fact the case. This optical illusion was indeed part of their aesthetic function.

The oldest stone-carved choir we know of is that of the cathedral of Santiago de Compostela; fragments of it, made by Master Mateo and his pupils in the second half of the twelfth century, have survived. In Toledo, the fourteenth-century stone enclosure remains, but in 1489 Rodrigo Alemán was commissioned to carve the panels decorating the lower choir stalls: these scenes are highly realistic, being incidents in the conquest of Granada. These events, whose outcome affected the whole of Spanish life, were rendered by the northern sculptor—a German, as his name indicates —with tremendous plastic energy. Crowded battle scenes are represented, with footsoldiers and mounted men storming the city, and the actual surrender of Granada is recorded in other scenes. Although the fortified city walls were not copied directly from life (there seems to be an element of fantasy here), the figures, both Christian and Moorish, are treated with commendable realism. It all looks as if the artist were panting to hear the news, so as to set it down immediately: the panels were completed in 1494, only two years after the conquest of Granada. Although Rodrigo Alemán was not the only master to specialize in relief sculpture (some years earlier, Juan de Malinas had carved the choir of León cathedral), no other was so prolific, and fine examples of his style can be seen at Zamora, Ciudad Rodrigo and Plasencia.

A number of tombs in Toledo are adorned with sculptures that show the characteristic naturalism of Late Gothic. The cathedral contains some beautiful tombs, such as that of Don Álvaro de Luna and his wife, in the middle of a magnificent chapel. But the most sensitive and delicate work of this group is the tomb of a knight who died young in the war with Granada: this is not in Toledo itself, though in the same artistic area—in the Santa Catalina chapel of Sigüenza cathedral. Here, Don Martín Vázquez de Arce, whose life was cut short at the age of twenty-five as he was helping "certain people of Jaén, in the plain of Granada," as the long epitaph puts it, is shown reclining, with his squire at his feet gazing at him in sorrow. In this moving work, the artist has wisely avoided any excess of decoration, and, in some mysterious way, the attitude and grouping of the figures seems to suggest Etruscan origins. The handling of forms

GIL DE SILOE (ACTIVE 1486-1499): TOMB OF THE INFANTE DON ALFONSO. 1486-1493. ALABASTER.
CARTHUSIAN MONASTERY OF MIRAFLORES, BURGOS.

GIL DE SILOE (ACTIVE 1486-1499): TOMB OF KING JOHN II AND QUEEN ISABELLA OF PORTUGAL. 1486-1493. ALABASTER.
CARTHUSIAN MONASTERY OF MIRAFLORES, BURGOS.

CATHEDRAL OF PALENCIA: RETROCHOIR. 16TH CENTURY.

and drapery folds, the delineation of facial features, and other details are wholly in the Gothic tradition. On the other hand, the ornamentation on the front of the sarcophagus, with plant motifs unfolding symmetrically around stems, seems to herald the coming of the Renaissance.

Moving from Toledo to Burgos, in the heart of Castile, we find a parallel development taking place throughout the second half of the fifteenth century. Active in Burgos in the middle years of the century was Juan de Colonia (John of Cologne), who crowned the cathedral towers with pointed spires. Thus began that series of alterations in the upper parts of the cathedral which resulted in a combination of two styles, one on top of the other. Juan's son Simón, who was born in Burgos, built the Chapel of

PORTAL OF THE COLLEGE OF SAN GREGORIO, VALLADOLID. 16TH CENTURY,

The grille closing off the nave in the church of the Carthusian monastery of El Paular is a fine example of the way in which ironwork grating had developed in Spain by the second half of the fifteenth century. It was made by Fray Francisco de Salamanca in the last decade of the century, and its decorative style reflects the prevailing Flamboyant Gothic of the period. The iron bars, placed vertically in two groups, are enriched with various ornaments, culminating in the upper part or cresting, with its graceful design of openwork rings arranged in intersecting circles. These forms are clearly of Mudejar origin. This marks the highest point of development of these wrought iron grilles, which had come a long way from their modest beginnings in Romanesque art in the form of iron lattices protecting church windows. From the thirteenth century on, grilles enclosing chapels and choirs became a distinctive feature of Spanish churches. The Gothic can be seen evolving into the Renaissance style almost without a break in the work of such masters as Francisco de Villalpando and Cristóbal de Andino, who left magnificent grilles in the cathedrals of Toledo and Burgos.

FRAY FRANCISCO DE SALAMANCA (ACTIVE 1493-1547): WROUGHT IRON GRILLE IN THE CARTHUSIAN MONASTERY OF EL PAULAR, NEAR MADRID. LATE 15TH CENTURY.

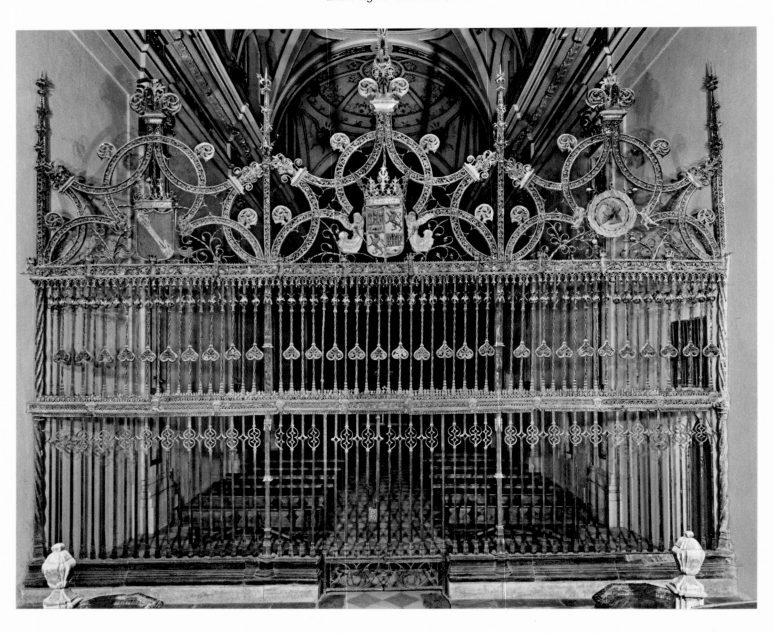

the Constable, at the time of the war with Granada, while its founder (who died a few days after the city was taken) was fighting the Moors. With its ogee arches, its cusping, its great coats of arms, its pinnacles, its starred vault with skylights in it to make it look lighter, the Chapel of the Constable rivals that of Don Álvaro de Luna in Toledo cathedral, and is even more original.

The hispanicization and artistic development of the Colonia family was continued by Francisco, Simón's son, who carved one of the portals of Burgos cathedral in a style that is already that of the Renaissance. But the Gothic spirit lingered on in Burgos for a good while yet, and as late as the mid-sixteenth century Juan de Vallejo imitated the structure of the Constable's Chapel when he built—with Renaissance details however—the great dome over the transept.

Sculpture in Burgos reached its highest level at the end of the fifteenth century, in the work of the Flemish master Gil de Siloe. He came from Antwerp and it appears that he had been in Castile from 1486. His masterpieces were made for the Carthusian monastery of Miraflores, newly built by Juan and Simón de Colonia. The Miraflores altarpiece is Gil de Siloe's most original and elaborate piece of sculpture. The richness of its carving is set off by the tombs Siloe made in front of it. On a starshaped tomb lie the figures of King John II and his wife Isabella of Portugal, parents of the Catholic Queen, while on the left is the praying figure of the Infante Don Alfonso; if he had lived, he would have reigned instead of his sister, and the union of Castile and Aragon would not have been achieved. These alabaster tombs confirm once more Siloe's obsession with fine points of detail. He was, indeed, a virtuoso of relief carving, embellishing his work with touch after touch of ornamental detail; perhaps he gave these minutiae the attention other artists concentrate on the faces, which in the Miraflores tombs are scarcely individualized.

Gil de Siloe's style had a profound impact on the whole region around Burgos: his activity there made it an art center whose influence dominated the neighboring provinces. That influence is quite obvious in the College of San Gregorio in Valladolid, where the façade, decorated with an opulence rivalling that of the most ornamental altarpiece, has many features that seem to have been taken from the Miraflores tombs. On the other hand, Simón de Colonia must have intervened in the design of the portal and courtyard, and here the styles of the two artists were combined. The college of Valladolid, which was founded by Alonso de Burgos, contains certain elements that prefigure the Renaissance. In contrast with the figures of savages decorating the door-posts, still distinctly Gothic in spirit, stands the main theme over the doorway, already imbued with Renaissance humanism: small naked boys, who look like Italian putti, are climbing among the branches of a pomegranate tree. This is undoubtedly an allusion to the conquest of Granada (which in Spanish means pomegranate) by the Catholic Kings only a few years before.

PEDRO COMPTE (?-1506): INTERIOR OF THE SILK EXCHANGE (LONJA), VALENCIA. 1482-1498.

The transition from Gothic to Renaissance art is illustrated even more strikingly in the retrochoir of Palencia cathedral. Begun by Don Alonso de Burgos (who had founded the College of San Gregorio at Valladolid), the retrochoir was completed by a bishop of Palencia, a member of the Fonseca family, who afterwards became bishop of Burgos. This helps to explain the artistic links between the three cities, here crystallized in a work that belongs to the early years of the sixteenth century. The complex ensemble of the sculptured retrochoir of Palencia, which closes off the choir of the cathedral from the central nave, is richly adorned with Flamboyant motifs; there are canopies topped with pinnacles, coats of arms with an ornamental as well as a heraldic value (the arms of the Catholic Kings, with the yoke and the arrows, are enclosed in a fanciful cusped arch), and to crown it all there is an elaborate cresting, which recalls that along the top of Gothic altar screens and grilles. Yet other motifs suggest the new art of the Renaissance: the side doors with semicircular arches, some small niches with scallop-shell conches, and the great frieze combining northern ornaments with others of Roman origin. The Palencia retrochoir is symbolic of this period of contrasts which ended with the reign of the Catholic Kings.

Southward, in Andalusia, which now formed part of the kingdom of Castile, further innovations were being made. At Seville an artist from Brittany, Lorenzo Mercadante, was using an unusual material in his monumental decorations: terracotta. Several figures on the cathedral façade are very nobly and realistically modelled in this material, which was malleable enough to let him concentrate all his attention on a lifelike rendering of each figure, and Mercadante penetrated with remarkable insight into the complex world of psychological characterization and individual expression. In the tympanum of the west door of Seville cathedral he represented the Nativity with a marvellous feeling of reality. A woman walks towards the manger, carrying gifts and laughing gaily. Mercadante's powers of apt and lifelike expression are seen at their best in such details as this.

Other northern artists worked on the decoration of the great Gothic cathedral in Seville. To one of them, Dancart, we owe the design of the main altarpiece, a work of colossal dimensions—the largest in the world. Arranged, as usual, in a number of tiers, panels and divisions, it is distinguished by the regularity of its layout: forming a vast rectangle, the altarpiece contains twenty-eight main scenes carved in relief, illustrating the life of Christ. Begun in 1482 by Dancart, it was not finished until 1525 by another artist, Jorge Fernández.

The great altarpieces of Castile which we have been considering show a variety of design that is characteristic of this type of work. At the same time they all have one thing in common: the profusion of their decoration. The churches of Aragon, too, contain some remarkable altarpieces of this period. One of the most original is illustrated here: the main altarpiece in the cathedral of Saragossa.

Architecture and sculpture in the second half of the fifteenth century did not develop in Aragon as they had done in Castile. Circumstances in the dominions of Ferdinand the Catholic were very different. Political and economic links had long since been forged with Italy, and fewer northern artists were led to settle in Aragon than in central Spain. There are, however, a number of works that reveal the interaction here of various art trends, and the most representative is the Lonja or Silk Exchange in Valencia, built in the last two decades of the fifteenth century by Pedro Compte. As we have seen, the interior was inspired by that of the Lonja at Palma, in Majorca, the vaults being supported by rows of cylindrical piers decorated with twisted flutings. But at Valencia the structure of the vaulting is more complicated than at Palma. On the outside, and in an additional section on one side (where there is a hall with a richly carved and panelled ceiling) Flamboyant ogee arches and traceries are found side by side with turrets and round bas-reliefs of Italian origin.

These two works—the main altarpiece of Saragossa cathedral and the Silk Exchange of Valencia—are characteristic examples of Aragonese sculpture and architecture in the second half of the fifteenth century; still others could be adduced to show how Italian forms were penetrating the art of Aragon. But before the full triumph of the Renaissance, painting in eastern Spain had a period of great splendor, thanks to the presence there of several artists schooled in the north, who developed the Flemish style introduced by Luis Dalmau. The outstanding name is that of the Catalan painter Jaime Huguet, who was born about 1415 and died in 1492; his documented works belong to the last four decades of his life.

The realism so powerfully expressed in the work of Jan van Eyck took a very personal turn in the work of Huguet. He was a great portrait painter, giving an intensely individualized likeness of each of his sitters. But he also loved a certain richness of effect, and this led him to use embossed gold in the haloes and crowns of his figures, and in the backgrounds and clothes. His lavishness in this respect appears most clearly in the altarpiece of St Augustine in Barcelona museum, particularly in the scene representing the saint's consecration. Augustine is portrayed in front view, full length, standing with his hands clasped in prayer while two prelates, symmetrically arranged on either side of him, put on his mitre; others, to right and left, maintain the rhythm and symmetry of the composition. The rich costumes and ornaments worn by the assembled bishops gave Huguet the opportunity for a splendid display of goldwork. The essentially Spanish qualities of this fine artist grew more and more marked in the course of his long life, as he evolved from the International Style of Bernardo Martorell and assimilated the innovations of Flemish art without ever losing his own personality.

Catalonia was fortunate in attracting a painter who left his mark in many different parts of Spain: this was Bartolomé Bermejo. From Cordova, where he was born, it is possible to follow his path through Saragossa and Valencia until he appears in Barcelona

JAIME HUGUET (ABOUT 1415-1492): ST VINCENT AT THE STAKE. PANEL OF THE SARRIÁ ALTARPIECE. MID-15TH CENTURY.
MUSEUM OF CATALAN ART, BARCELONA.

JAIME JACOMART (1410-1461): THE VIRGIN AND CHILD WITH ST ANNE. CENTRAL PANEL OF THE ALTARPIECE OF CALIXTUS III. ABOUT 1450.
COLLEGIATE CHURCH, JÁTIVA (VALENCIA).

BARTOLOMÉ BERMEJO (?-AFTER 1498): ABBOT ST DOMINIC OF SILOS. ABOUT 1477. PRADO, MADRID.

in 1490, when he signed the Pietà still preserved in the cathedral. In the first study to be made of Bermejo's work, published in 1926, Elías Tormo described him as the most robust and vigorous of the Spanish Primitives, and although we now know much more about medieval painting, this opinion still holds. In all his work Bermejo's energetic character is plain, and so is his Flemish background. In the panel representing St Dominic of Silos in the Prado, one is struck by the commanding figure of this richly dressed, bejewelled man who looks straight before him, and quelled by his unwavering gaze in a face modelled with geometrical regularity—this in spite of the artist's painstaking attention to details that might have distracted the eye of the spectator. In the Pietà in Barcelona cathedral, with St Jerome on one side and the donor, Canon Desplá, on the other, one is struck above all by the dramatic gesture of the Virgin holding the dead Christ in her arms; and the kneeling figure of the donor is clearly a magnificent portrait made from life. The anecdotes depicted in the landscape background do nothing to detract from the plastic vigor of the figures.

These two painters, Huguet and Bermejo, between them display some of the most noteworthy characteristics of late fifteenth-century painting in Aragon. But each part of the kingdom—Aragon proper, Catalonia, Valencia, Majorca—had its own artistic circles with masters whose work has an individual stamp, and in many of them Flemish and Italian elements are mingled. Documents from the archives of the period mention the names of many native painters, but there were plenty of foreigners too, who, with their checkered background, often combined the most disparate tendencies. A representative case is that of the German master Anye Bru (as he is called in Spain, his real name being Hans or Heinrich Brün or Brunn). In 1502 he painted an altarpiece for the monastery of San Cugat del Vallés, near Barcelona. The scene of the saint's beheading has a terrible realism. It has been pointed out, quite rightly, that this overstrained heightening of dramatic effect is not a Spanish characteristic, in spite of what is often supposed. Some details are so Italianate that the panel can really be considered to qualify as a Renaissance painting. In any case, it is yet another sign of the ferment of contending styles in Spanish art at the beginning of the sixteenth century.

Painting in Castile shows the impact of Flemish art more extensively than it does in Aragon. Panel paintings imported from the Low Countries were from the first very highly esteemed in Castile, and Queen Isabella herself formed a large collection of them, the remains of which survive in the Royal Chapel in Granada and the Royal Palace in Madrid. And besides pictures by the great Flemish masters, Flemish artists themselves came to Spain, not only sculptors and architects but painters of high ability like Jorge Inglés and Juan de Flandes. Spanish artists must have visited the Low Countries too. Thus a vigorous Hispano-Flemish school arose, and although national characteristics often prevail in the work of members of this school, they all based their art on the great achievements of the fifteenth-century Flemish masters, such as Jan van Eyck.

ANYE BRU: THE MARTYRDOM OF ST CUCUFAT. 1502-1506. PANEL OF THE ALTARPIECE OF SAN CUGAT DEL VALLÉS (BARCELONA).
MUSEUM OF CATALAN ART, BARCELONA.

FERNANDO GALLEGO (ACTIVE 1468-1507): THE MARTYRDOM OF ST CATHERINE. PRADO, MADRID.

The artist who best shows how Flemish art was assimilated in Spain is Fernando Gallego, who worked actively over a wide area centering on Salamanca. His life is documented between 1468 and 1507, and so it coincides with the reign of the Catholic Kings. As his work clearly reflects some knowledge of several northern painters, it has been supposed, reasonably enough, that he must have been trained in the Low Countries; he also seems to have had contacts with German artists like Konrad Witz and Martin Schongauer. Another source of his style is to be found in a work with which he must have been familiar: the altarpiece in the old cathedral of Salamanca, painted about the middle of the fifteenth century by Nicolás Florentino. Even more strikingly than his contemporaries, Gallego testifies to the curious mixture of styles characteristic of Spanish art at the end of the Middle Ages.

His Martyrdom of St Catherine, recently acquired by the Prado, is a painting that seeks to condense a scene full of movement. It represents the first episode of the martyrdom, when the wheel on which the saint's body is to be broken is suddenly destroyed by angels descending from heaven with swords and an axe. Several of her torturers have fallen to the ground, while others gaze in awe at the miracle. The background is a conventional landscape with a river and a city—a stock motif in Flemish pictures. Here, as in his other paintings, Gallego likes to show figures and objects in foreshortening, dwells on rich decorative effects (the brocaded cloak of the standing figure on the left, for instance), and carries expressiveness to the point of caricature (as in the gestures of the man on the right who is falling to the ground). In addition to these elements, the picture contains a feature which, for that time and place, was highly unusual: St Catherine is represented in the nude, her sharply drawn figure being of Gothic rather than Renaissance design. The figure of Eve in an altarpiece in Zamora cathedral appears to be the first representation of a naked woman in Spanish painting. But in Fernando Gallego's picture of St Catherine this nakedness is unnecessary, as is proved by another painting of her, documented as the work of Francisco Gallego (yet also showing the hand of Fernando, who must have been either his father or brother). We may take it, then, that the nude in the Prado panel was treated for its own sake, no doubt under the influence of Italian painters, who were already showing a keen interest in the nude.

At Salamanca, with its great university (where the spirit of Renaissance humanism had already taken root), Fernando Gallego was given a magnificent opportunity to develop a theme which had not previously been dealt with in Spanish mural painting: the sky with the constellations, interpreted in the classical manner, which he painted on a vaulted ceiling in the university library. Unfortunately only a third of the composition survives: the sun and Mercury in his chariot, Virgo as a winged female figure, Sagittarius as a centaur with his bow drawn, the Herdsman as a hybrid with a bull's body and human arms and head. These scenes, however, are more than enough to show the interest then felt in such subjects. It has been suggested by Laínez Alcalá

FERNANDO GALLEGO (ACTIVE 1468-1507): THE SKY WITH THE CONSTELLA

One of the most interesting fresco sequences to come down to us from the period of the Catholic Kings was installed a few years ago in a room giving on the court-yard of the Escuelas Menores of the University of Salamanca. This vast composition, only part of which has survived, was the work of Fernando Gallego, possibly with the help of Pedro Berruguete (as Laínez Alcalá has suggested). The personified

...OUT 1500. FRESCO. ESCUELAS MENORES, UNIVERSITY OF SALAMANCA.

constellations and the mythological allusions give an Italianate overtone to a painting that technically still shows Flemish influence. The details of Apollo's quadriga and Mercury's chariot, drawn by eagles, are in the Renaissance style, whereas the figure of Virgo above them, with its sharply folded draperies, is linked more closely with the Gothic tradition.

227

MASTER OF ÁVILA: TRIPTYCH OF THE NATIVITY. ABOUT 1473. MUSEUM OF THE LÁZARO-GALDIANO FOUNDATION, MADRID.

that this work may represent the horoscope of the prince Don Juan, the unfortunate heir of the Catholic Kings, who died very young at Salamanca in 1497: if this were so, the prince's destiny would have to be seen in astrological terms. The strange mixture of pagan elements at a time when life was pervaded by religious misgivings is not really surprising: in so much else, myth and religion were combined.

The best example of pagan and Christian elements used side by side, indeed amalgamated, is a very interesting tapestry in Toledo cathedral, probably woven in the second half of the fifteenth century, possibly at Arras. The whole thing is full of symbols. The Creator, embodied in a figure that personifies agility, turns a crank-handle that sets in motion a celestial sphere where the signs of the Zodiac unfold around the Pole Star. Atlas also helps to push the sphere, and on the right there is a curious composition consisting of Virgil, Astrology, Arithmetic and Philosophy. A Latin text in Gothic letters inscribed on the tapestry seeks to give unity to all these disparate ideas. Some such text as this may have been the source on which Fernando Gallego drew in painting his "sky" in the university library of Salamanca. Other works of his can be seen in Ciudad Rodrigo, Toro, Zamora, and Burgos.

In and around Ávila, in Castile, worked another artist of note who is known as the Master of Ávila—possibly to be identified with a painter named García del Barco, who was active between 1465 and 1473 and had professional contacts with Fernando Gallego in Salamanca. A magnificent triptych by this master is preserved at the Lázaro-Galdiano Foundation in Madrid. The central panel represents the Adoration of the Child with the Virgin, St Joseph and a donor; the side panels show the angel bringing the tidings to the shepherds and the Wise Men watching the star of Bethlehem. When the folding panels are closed, the triptych shows the Annunciation in grisaille. The style of this work has the characteristic features of Hispano-Flemish art. The firmness of the drawing appears particularly in the energetic rendering of the drapery folds, in which the artist keeps to the practice of the German masters. The faces, though individualized, are rather coarse. A typically Spanish note is added by the sumptuous costumes, especially those of the three Wise Men. The landscape is wholly in the tradition of Flemish painting, although more emphasis is laid on anecdotal elements, such as the animals in the scene with the shepherds, or the figures in the other wing of the triptych who, standing on some hillocks, are watching an over-sized star enclosing the figure of the Christ Child bearing the cross on his shoulder. With his direct and expressive style, the Master of Ávila marks a further development of that Hispano-Flemish art which, initiated in Castile by Jorge Inglés, reached its final form with Juan de Flandes, who worked in the region around Palencia and was also in the service of Isabella the Catholic.

Other anonymous masters, as well as those whose names we know or whose work is easily identified, show how the Hispano-Flemish style spread through the kingdom of Castile. Among these was the painter of the panel portraying the Catholic Kings, in the Prado. Few works have a more serene and orderly composition, though it is slightly monotonous. At the back of a large room, on a Gothic throne, sits the Virgin with the Child; in the foreground, in the center of two groups, are Ferdinand and Isabella, kneeling in an attitude of prayer. The king is surrounded by the prince Don Juan, the inquisitor Torquemada and St Thomas, who stands holding a model of the Church on a book and a phylactery in his hand; the queen is surrounded by Doña Juana and the chronicler Peter Martyr of Anglería, both kneeling (the latter with a knife at his breast to recall his patron saint), and St Dominic of Guzmán standing, holding a book, some long-stemmed white lilies, and a phylactery. Iconographically, this painting is extremely valuable, but stylistically it gives a rather one-sided idea of Spanish art in the reign of the Catholic Kings, for there is no sign in it of that blending of Gothic and Renaissance trends which chiefly characterizes the art of this period.

About 1490, when this panel was painted, the links connecting Spanish art with Italy were being drawn closer by a great artist, with results destined to be decisive for the future. This was Pedro Berruguete, whose personality is extraordinarily attractive

The tapestry of the Celestial Sphere, the Astrolabes and the Signs of the Zodiac belongs to Toledo cathedral and since 1958 has been exhibited in the Santa Cruz Museum. Some 26 feet in length and 13½ feet high, it is decorated with a vast array of figures and themes: they illustrate that confusion between sacred and profane motifs which is characteristic of so much fifteenth-century art. Some of the subjects—the Constellations, Virgil with three symbols of the Liberal Arts (Astrology, Arithmetic and Philosophy), and figures as unrelated as Atlas and God the Father (as Supreme Power)—show how humanistic currents from Italy had penetrated into Flanders and Northern France, where this tapestry was woven.

TAPESTRY OF THE CELESTIAL SPHERE, THE ASTROLABES AND THE SIGNS OF THE ZODIAC. MID-15TH CENTURY. MUSEUM OF SANTA CRUZ, TOLEDO (PROPERTY OF TOLEDO CATHEDRAL).

and whose temperament and circumstances seem to make him the most representative Spanish painter of his day. He was born at Paredes de Nava, near Palencia, became familiar with the art of the Hispano-Flemish masters in his youth and felt its effect profoundly. But when he went to Italy, some time before 1477, to work on the decoration of the library in the ducal palace at Urbino, the influences on him changed. In Italy he collaborated with a Flemish painter, Justus of Ghent, and thus had the strange experience of being with an artist who was developing the style he had known in Spain in a country where the ideals of the ancient world were being enthusiastically revived by artists and scholars. Even today it has not been unanimously agreed which part of the decoration of the Urbino library was the work of which painter, but critics are now inclined to think Berruguete painted the *studiolo* or small study. The Liberal Arts and the group of Duke Federico of Urbino and his court are surely by Berruguete. The latter scene, dominated by the Duke and his son, is painted in a setting that is fully Renaissance. Berruguete knew how to reflect his surroundings, though a Spanish energy appears in the expressive strength of the faces.

After returning to Castile, Berruguete worked in Palencia, Burgos and Ávila. The pictures painted there show all the elements that entered into his previous experience. He was careful to emphasize the effects of perspective, conveyed in the checkered pattern of floor tiles or in the receding lines of a wall. His architectural motifs are usually in the Renaissance style, with pilasters, columns and Roman arches. But the expression of facial features and attitudes, the vigorous rendering of drapery folds, and other details as well, all reflect the Flemish basis of his training. Yet for all these foreign ingredients, his personality remains thoroughly Spanish. His realism goes further than that of the Flemish masters; it appears in a direct and spontaneous language that sacrifices correctness of form for an immediate impact on the beholder. This means that his occasional lapses and carelessness are more than atoned for by the strength and feeling of his painting. Like so many other Spanish painters, Berruguete was archaic in his persistent use of gold backgrounds (sometimes, as an exception, he used silver) to achieve a sense of richness; this was the case in the panels he made for the Palencia altarpiece, which were later repainted with landscapes. In the same way he did not hesitate to include Mudejar ceilings in his pictures, combining them with Renaissance elements. The contemporary of Fernando Gallego, whom he predeceased, in 1504, Berruguete was the greatest of the Castilian painters who introduced the Renaissance into Spain. His adoption of the new art forms gaining currency in Spain was approved by the monarchs and encouraged by the patronage of great families like the Mendozas and Fonsecas.

The gradual introduction of the Renaissance was one of the most complex developments in the history of Spanish art, since a number of factors worked for it, and a number against it. At a time when national unity, centered on religious unity, was being forged, the atmosphere prevailing in Italy, where the ancient world was often exalted

PEDRO BERRUGUETE (ABOUT 1450-1504): KING SOLOMON, DETAIL OF THE SANTA EULALIA ALTARPIECE. ABOUT 1480.
PARISH CHURCH OF SANTA EULALIA, PAREDES DE NAVA (PALENCIA).

at the expense of the Christian faith, was bound to arouse suspicion. If Savonarola in fifteenth-century Florence felt called upon to defend medieval orthodoxy against the Medici and the Pope, it is hardly surprising that the humanistic ideas met opposition in Spain. But there was no lack of enthusiastic supporters for the Renaissance, too, and the most illustrious families were among them.

The Mendoza family was ahead of all others. Don Iñigo de Mendoza, Marquis of Santillana (1398-1458), as we have seen composed sonnets "in the Italian style" at the court of King John II of Castile. Among his children were Doña Mencía, who was attached to the Gothic style and sponsored the construction of the Chapel of the Constable in Burgos cathedral, and Don Pedro, Archbishop of Toledo and Grand Cardinal of Spain. The latter, who died in 1495, favored the Renaissance style and undertook buildings that launched Spanish architecture in a new direction. In his service was Lorenzo Vázquez, who designed the main doorway of the College of Santa Cruz in Valladolid: this work marks the beginning of Renaissance architecture in Spain. Other buildings were owed to Don Pedro's patronage or to that of close relations of his who followed his example. Admittedly, his nephew, the Duke of Infantado, called in Juan Guas, an exponent of Late Gothic, when he built his palace at Guadalajara; but in the convents of the Piedad at Guadalajara and Mondéjar, and in the Medinaceli Palace at Cogolludo, the new art of the Renaissance was triumphant. A grandson of the Marquis of Santillana, the Count of Tendilla, was Castilian ambassador to Rome and was given a fine sword with Renaissance decoration on it by the pope in 1486. Elías Tormo was right in saying that "this weapon opened up the breach for the entry of the Renaissance into Spain."

It was the Count of Tendilla who brought to Spain the great Milanese humanist Peter Martyr of Anglería, and in Granada, where he was governor of the Alhambra, the Count maintained his love of letters and the arts until his death in 1515. In the territory newly conquered from the Moors, another Mendoza had his estates: he was the son of the Great Cardinal (who, like the good Renaissance prelate he was, had his human weaknesses, one of which involved offspring), who built the castle of Lacalahorra, with a splendid courtyard in the Renaissance style designed by Lorenzo Vázquez. The enlightened patronage of the Mendoza family, extending through several generations, provided a vital stimulus in the renewal of Spanish art.

The Fonseca family also played a significant part in the rise and—in spite of all resistance—ultimate triumph of Renaissance art. This large family, forming many branches, came originally from Galicia, and the five red stars of its coat of arms were to be found on monuments almost everywhere in the kingdom of Castile. One Fonseca built the castle of Coca; another, as bishop of Palencia and Burgos, undertook important work in the cathedrals of both cities. The Fonseca emblem appears on works of art and architecture in Toro, Alcalá de Henares, Toledo, Cordova and Seville.

But their main contribution to the development of the Renaissance in Spain was made by Don Alonso de Fonseca, Archbishop of Santiago de Compostela and Patriarch of Alexandria, who died in 1512, and by his son (born of his love affair with Doña María de Ulloa), also called Don Alonso, who became Archbishop of Santiago and Toledo. These two Fonsecas were instrumental in promoting and acclimatizing Renaissance art in Salamanca and Santiago de Compostela. The Ursuline convent in Salamanca, founded by Don Alonso the elder, was built in 1490, and the Renaissance decoration in its interior is a few years earlier than that of the College of Santa Cruz in Valladolid. Don Alonso the younger became a prominent member of the court of Charles V and a friend of Erasmus of Rotterdam. He followed his father's example and helped to make Salamanca one of the most beautiful Renaissance cities of Spain.

And what, in this time of change, was the attitude of the Catholic Kings? The French scholar Emile Bertaux introduced the term "Isabelline style" to designate the Flamboyant Gothic architecture that made its appearance in Spain during the last third of the fifteenth century. But did Queen Isabella feel no attraction for the art forms that were coming from Italy? Certainly she did; and Sánchez Cantón has accordingly made serious objections to Bertaux's term. While the queen was alive the Italian artist Niccolo Pisano decorated the chapel of the Alcázar in Seville with Renaissance tiles, and her attachment to the Mendoza family must have helped to form her taste in matters of art. But undoubtedly the much more dominant role was played by the king, who was politically much interested in Italian affairs and temperamentally was always receptive to new ideas. Ferdinand, who as an administrator was careful almost to the point of meanness, cannot go down to history as a great patron of the arts, but he certainly showed his preference for the Renaissance style in a definite way. Between the queen's death in 1504 and the king's in 1516, the great change took place at court level.

Like others, including Cardinal Mendoza, Ferdinand the Catholic gave commissions for Renaissance tombs. We know that the Tuscan sculptor from Settignano, Domenico Fancelli, who had been brought to Spain by the Mendoza family, went to Granada in 1511 to see a portrait of the prince Don Juan, which was to serve him as a model for the figure of the prince on his tomb in Santo Tomás in Ávila. The king must have been pleased with the tomb, which was finished in 1512, because two years later Fancelli ordered marble from Carrara for a great cenotaph in the Royal Chapel at Granada. This work was not finished until 1517, a year after the king's death, but the Renaissance figures of the Catholic Kings, dominating a structure in the Gothic style (which was already out of date at the time and to Charles V seemed paltry), may be the best symbol of the new direction Spanish art was taking when the reign of the Emperor began.

INDEX OF NAMES AND PLACES

LIST OF ILLUSTRATIONS

ON THE THRESHOLD OF ART

THE TRIUMPH OF THE EAST IN THE WEST

SPAIN'S INTEGRATION IN EUROPE

THIS BOOK WAS DESIGNED AND PRODUCED BY THE TECHNICAL
STAFF OF EDITIONS D'ART ALBERT SKIRA. FINISHED THE TENTH
DAY OF AUGUST NINETEEN HUNDRED AND SIXTY-SEVEN.

TEXT AND ILLUSTRATIONS PRINTED BY THE

COLOR STUDIOS
IMPRIMERIES RÉUNIES, LAUSANNE.

COLOR PLATES ENGRAVED BY GUEZELLE & RENOUARD, PARIS

BLACK AND WHITE PLATES BY ROTO-SADAG S.A., GENEVA

All the photographs in this book are by
MAURICE BABEY, BASEL

*except those on the following pages: page 71 (Henry B. Beville, Alexandria, Virginia),
pages 155, 156 (Hans Hinz, Basel), page 175 (Casa Truyol, Palma, Majorca). Line drawings
by courtesy of Martín Almagro (page 28), E. Hernández Pacheco (page 29), Magín Berenguer
(page 138), and Kenneth J. Conant (page 148).*

PRINTED IN SWITZERLAND